BOUTIQUE
WIRE JEWELRY

STACKPOLE
BOOKS

Published by Stackpole Books
An imprint of The Rowman & Littlefield Publishing Group, Inc.
4501 Forbes Boulevard, Suite 200
Lanham, Maryland 20706
www.stackpolebooks.com

Distributed by NATIONAL BOOK NETWORK
800-462-6420

Photography: Naohito Sakuma (Hibi Photography Office) and Akira Kojima
Model: Mizuki Shimojima
Planning: Keiichi Sugiyama (Taiho Trading Co., Ltd.)
Editor: Sayuri Tezuka (gris)

English Translation: Mayumi Anzai
English Language Editor: Lindsay Fair
Technical Editor: Denise Peck

We have made every effort to ensure the accuracy and completeness of these instructions. We cannot, however, be responsible for human error, typographical mistakes, or variations in individual work.

British Library Cataloguing in Publication Information available

Library of Congress Cataloging-in-Publication Data
Library of Congress Control Number: 2018967949

ISBN: 978-0-8117-3830-9 (paperback)
ISBN: 978-0-8117-6832-0 (electronic)

♾™ The paper used in this publication meets the minimum requirements of American National Standard for Information Sciences—Permanence of Paper for Printed Library Materials, ANSI/NISO Z39.48-1992.

Printed in China

BOUTIQUE
WIRE JEWELRY

Easy and elegant necklaces, bracelets, rings, and earrings

Yuko Shimojima and Miki Onuma

STACKPOLE
BOOKS

Guilford, Connecticut

Introduction

Wire is one of the most versatile materials jewelry makers can use. Its flexibility, both literally and figuratively, allows you to create almost any jewelry design your mind can conceive.
A single wire can become...

...A minimalist bracelet
...An elaborate embellishment
...A way to connect fancy gemstones and shiny beads

There are so many different techniques that can be used in wire jewelry making. In this book, we'll cover the basics, such as making head pins and eye pins, as well as a few more advanced techniques, including classic wire wrapping and wire crochet.

Our goal is to create a welcoming resource for beginners who are interested in working with wire for the first time, as well as a source of inspiration for jewelry making pros looking for fresh ideas—it's amazing how simple decisions, like changing the wire thickness or shape, can create exciting new designs.

We hope this book inspires you to develop a feel for working with wire and creating special jewelry pieces that you'll cherish forever.

—Yuko Shimojima and Miki Onuma

Contents

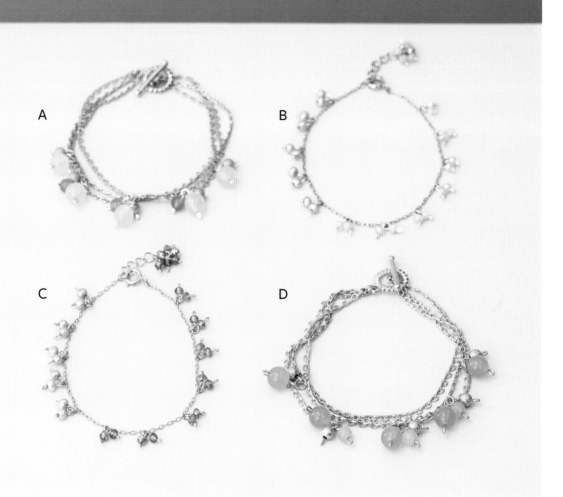

A

B

C

D

Beaded Charm Bracelets

These delicate bracelet designs feature small beads that sway elegantly as you move. You can choose any of your favorite beads: natural stones, cut glass, and metal beads will all work well. Designs A and D are composed of a variety of bead sizes and three separate chains for a layered look, while designs B and C showcase sets of pearl beads in a neutral color scheme for a subtle ombré effect.

INSTRUCTIONS ON PAGES 48 & 50

A

B

Coin Pearl Bracelet

This simple, yet classic bracelet design features Swarovski
coin pearls connected with eye pins.

INSTRUCTIONS ON PAGE 52

Faceted Rondelle Bracelet

This sophisticated bracelet features five faceted glass rondelle beads separated by dainty gold floral spacer beads. Add a faceted rondelle bead to the extender chain for an elegant touch.

INSTRUCTIONS ON PAGE 54

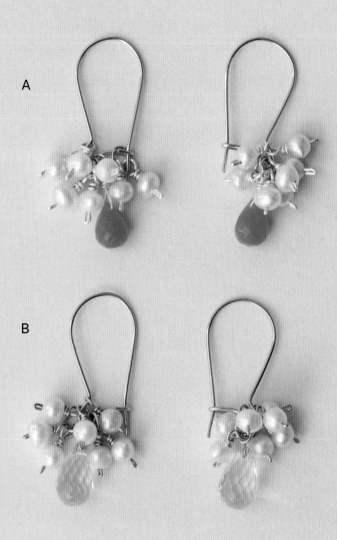

A

B

Pearl Dangle Earrings

These elegant earrings are made with potato pearls, freshwater pearls named for their irregular shapes. Add a beautiful stone briolette for a touch of glamour.

INSTRUCTIONS ON PAGE 56

Milk Glass Necklace (A & B) & Stacked Shell Necklace (C & D)

Use one large, uniquely-shaped bead for a dramatic impact or string a whole row of small, thin beads to create a layered look. Using wire wrapped loops makes it possible to connect to very fine chains.

INSTRUCTIONS ON PAGES 58 & 60

Gemstone Kaleidoscope Necklace

Wire wrapped loops are a great way to securely attach large beads. Create a bold design with natural stones and unique metal links.

INSTRUCTIONS ON PAGE 62

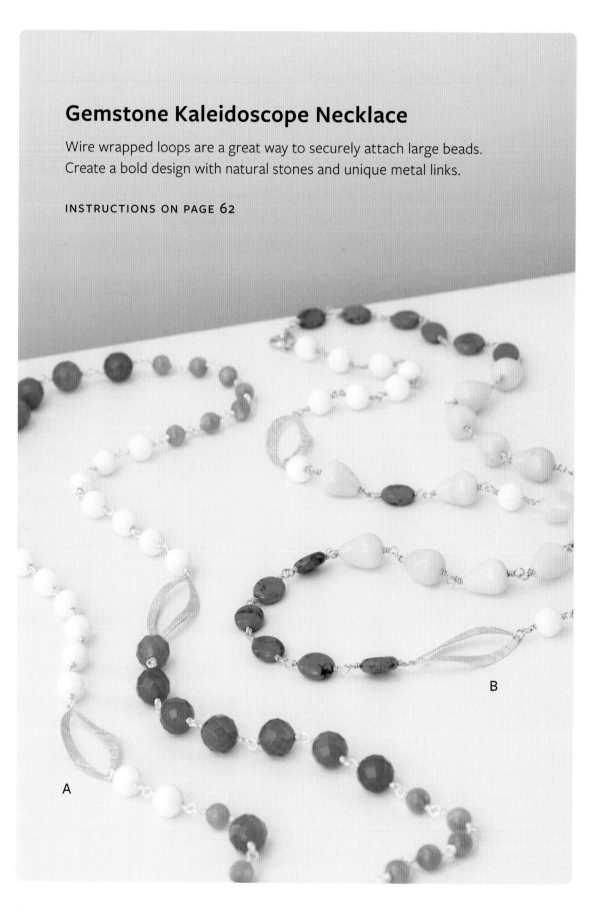

A

B

A

B

Double Strand Necklace

Delicate beads and wire wrapped loops combine to create this pretty layered necklace design. Use natural stone beads for a pop of color, or try freshwater pearls for a neutral look.

INSTRUCTIONS ON PAGE 64

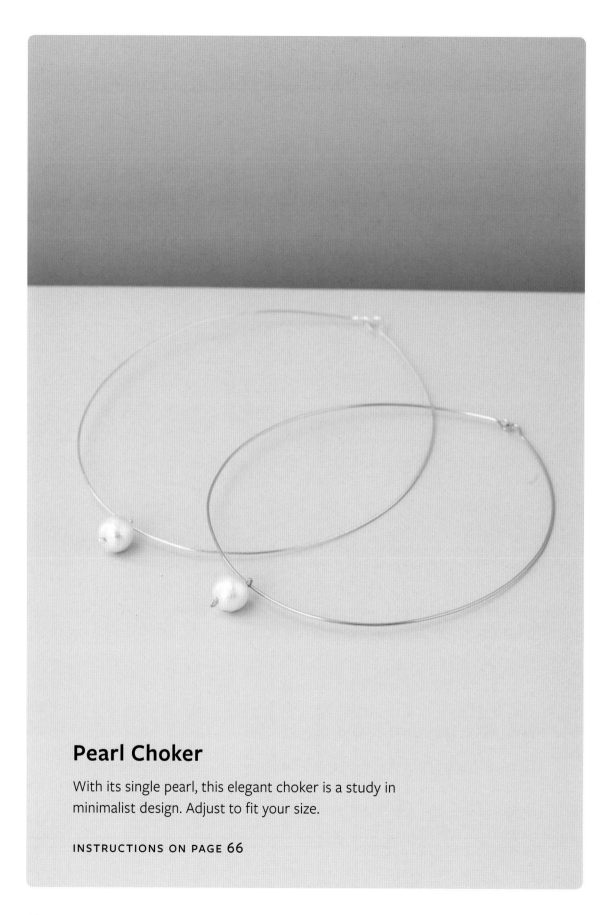

Pearl Choker

With its single pearl, this elegant choker is a study in minimalist design. Adjust to fit your size.

INSTRUCTIONS ON PAGE 66

B

A

Metal Bangle

Mixed metals and beads of varying sizes combine to create this chic bangle. The hook closure is ingeniously built right into the design of this bracelet.

INSTRUCTIONS ON PAGE 68

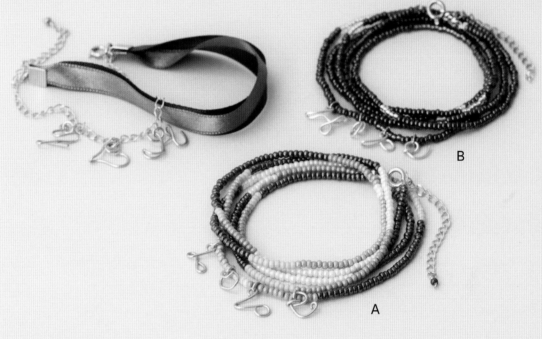

B

A

Charming Wrap Bracelets

Combine wire letters with different materials, like beads or ribbon, to spell out your name or a favorite word. The multi-strand design will help you achieve the boho layered look with just one simple bracelet. This versatile design can also be worn as a necklace.

INSTRUCTIONS ON PAGE 70

A

B

Mantra Necklaces

You can create complete words with a single wire, or layer a couple for a complete message! Add a small charm for a special touch.

INSTRUCTIONS ON PAGE 72

Lashed Bangles & Earrings

Have fun experimenting with different color combinations and patterns to create these simple beaded accessories. Seed beads and thin wire are wrapped around a thicker wire base using the lashing technique.

INSTRUCTIONS ON PAGES 74 & 76

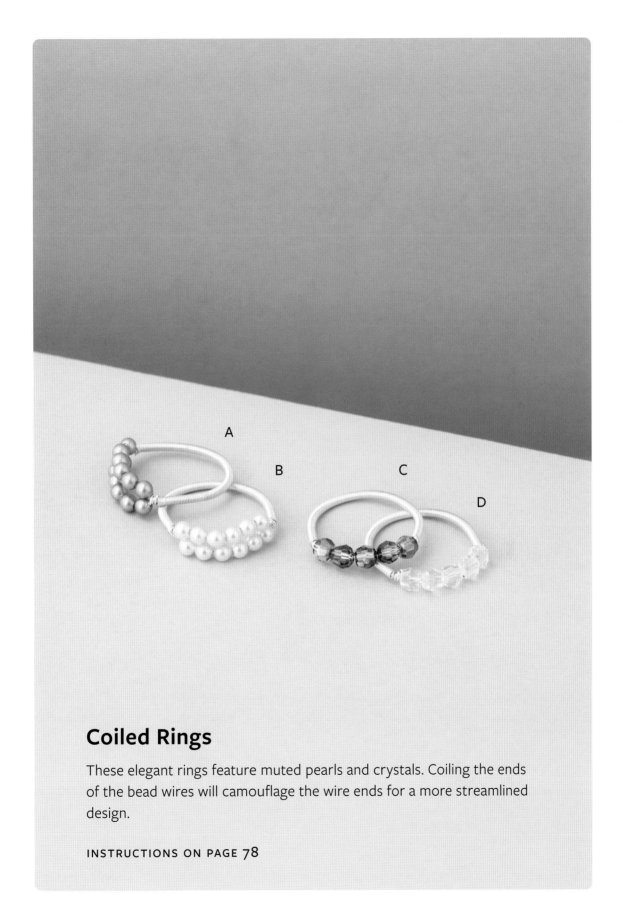

Coiled Rings

These elegant rings feature muted pearls and crystals. Coiling the ends of the bead wires will camouflage the wire ends for a more streamlined design.

INSTRUCTIONS ON PAGE 78

Pearl Nest Earrings

Attach a pearl in the middle of a crocheted nest of fine wire. Use a ball earring finding for a subtle dangle, or try adding some chains for a dramatic statement.

INSTRUCTIONS ON PAGE 80

C

A

B

Twisted Bangles & Flat Wire Rings

These pieces were designed to showcase the simple shape and texture of flat wire. It's important to select the right wire thickness to achieve the clean, modern look of these designs.

INSTRUCTIONS ON PAGES 82 AND 85

Wrapped Pendants

This technique allows you to make jewelry with cabochons, which are flat-backed, undrilled stones. Combine different colored wires for a unique look.

INSTRUCTIONS ON PAGES 90 & 95

Ribbon Pendant

This dainty design uses fancy square wires to create intricate detailing and a pretty bow shape. Tarnish resistant silver wire combines with white pearls for an elegant look.

INSTRUCTIONS ON PAGE 100

All About Wire

Used frequently in jewelry making, craft wire is copper wire with a permanent colored enamel coating that won't chip or crack. This type of wire is dead soft, which means it's malleable and can be used to create jewelry designs with bends and loops. Craft wire is available in a variety of colors, sizes, and shapes, and is sold in craft stores and online.

Color

Although craft wire is available in a rainbow of colors, the projects in this book are made with just a handful of classic metal shades. Some colors of craft wire are silver plated, which means they have a layer of pure silver between the copper wire and enamel coating, which adds a brilliant shine. Silver plated colors are noted with a *.

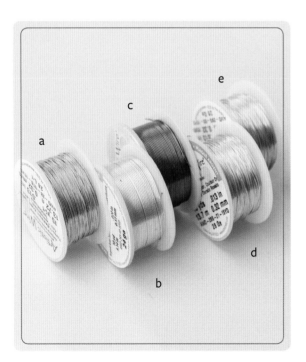

a. Tarnish resistant brass
Resembles 18kt gold.

b. Tarnish resistant silver*
Shiny, white silvery color wire that works well with sterling silver or silver findings.

c. Antique brass
Darkened brass that simulates antique metal. Formerly known as gun metal.

d. Rose gold*
Pinkish gold.

e. Gold color*
Resembles 14 kt gold.

- ✦ **Tinned copper:** Whitish color that is slightly darker and more gray than silver. Will patina over time.
- ✦ **Stainless steel:** Made of 304 grade stainless steel, this wire is tougher than copper wire. One advantage to stainless steel wire is that metal allergy is less likely to occur.

Size & Shape

To determine a wire's size, simply measure its diameter. In North America, wire size is measured in gauge, abbreviated as "ga" throughout this book, while in many European countries, wire size is measured in millimeters. It's important to remember that the larger the gauge number, the smaller the wire's diameter. For example, 30 gauge wire is thinner than 18 gauge wire. The following chart lists wire sizes commonly used in this book:

Gauge	18	20	22	24	26	28	30
Millimeters	1.02	0.81	0.64	0.51	0.40	0.32	0.25

Craft wire is available in many different shapes, but round wire is the most common wire shape used in jewelry making. As its name suggests, this type of wire has a circular cross section. Refer to page 28 for information on other types of wire used for the projects in this book.

Certain wire sizes and shapes are recommended for specific jewelry making techniques. You'll find this information listed in the technique guides throughout the book, as well as the materials lists for individual projects.

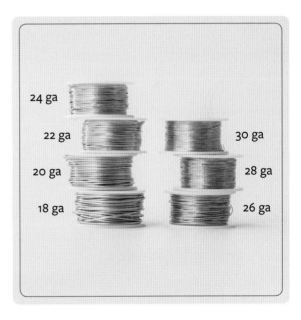

Other Wire Types

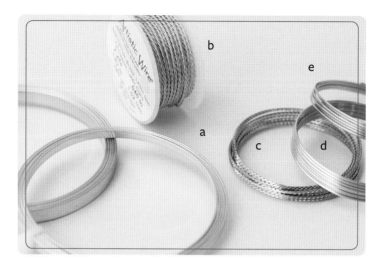

a. Flat wire

Available in 3 mm and 5 mm thicknesses, this harder wire will require stronger tools, such as bail making pliers.

b. Twisted wire

Three strands of craft wire are uniformly twisted together to create a unique texture. You can make your own stranded wire, but purchasing this type of wire will give your jewelry a professional look. Available in 18, 20, 22, and 24 ga.

c. Fancy square wire

Composed of three wires that are twisted together, then tooled to create a smooth, shiny surface, this wire is ideal for wrapping. Available in 20, 21, 22, and 24 ga.

d. Square wire

With its square cross section, this wire is often used as the base of wire wrapped designs and holds stones that will be banded with half round wire. Available in 20, 21, 22, and 24 ga.

e. Half round wire

This wire has a semicircular cross section and is often used for wrapping stones. The flat side of the wire is aligned with square wire, while the round side will be visible in the finished design. This process is known as banding.

Other Materials

In addition to wire, you'll need a few other jewelry components in order to make the designs in this book.

Findings

It's important to select the appropriate findings for your projects, as they will influence both the style and function of the finished piece.

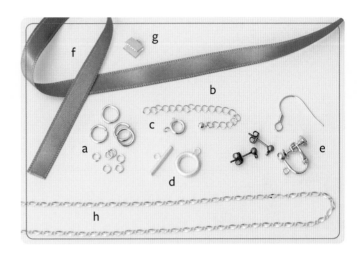

a. Round jump rings

Basic hardware used for connections. These are made with wire and consequently come in a variety of gauges, as well as diameters. Use jump rings appropriate to your projects.

b. Extender chain

Attaches to the end of a bracelet or necklace, making size adjustment possible.

c. Clasp

Fastener for a bracelet or necklace. A spring ring clasp is shown here, but other types are also used, such as lobster claw clasps.

d. Toggles

A toggle bar and a toggle ring combine for an alternate type of clasp.

e. Ear wires

Used for earrings, these come in a variety of types, such as French hooks, kidney wires, and lever back.

f. Ribbon

Suede and silk ribbons provide interesting contrast when combined with metal.

g. Crimp cord ends

Metal fittings for the ends of ribbon and leather cords. Please choose the size according to the width of the ribbon.

h. Chain

Some chains are made with openable links, others with closed links. The openable links can be shortened or lengthened and connected easily. Closed link chains require jump rings to connect.

Beads

When it comes to choosing beads, it may seem like the possibilities are nearly endless. We'll introduce the different types of beads used in this book, but choose your favorites.

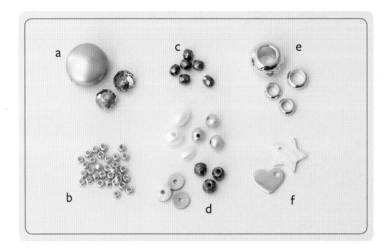

a. Swarovski crystal

Cut glass with brilliant sparkle. These beads come in a variety of shapes and sizes. Swarovski also makes glass pearls.

b. Seed beads

Small round beads available in several sizes and thousands of colors.

c. Czech glass beads

Relatively inexpensive glass beads available in a large variety of shapes and colors.

d. Natural stones

Freshwater pearls, shell beads, and gemstones often display irregular shapes and colors and can be used to create designs with organic appeal.

e. Metal beads

Metal beads come in a wide range of designs and can be shiny or matte, simple or intricately carved.

f. Charms

Available in all sorts of shapes and sizes. Use a round jump ring to connect a charm to your design.

It's also convenient to have bead mats and trays to corral your beads while you work.

Tools

You'll need some basic jewelry making tools, plus a few tools specifically designed for working with wire.

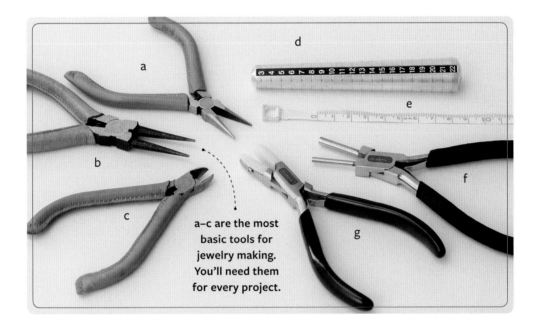

a–c are the most basic tools for jewelry making. You'll need them for every project.

a. Chain-nose pliers

Tapered jaws with smooth, flat surfaces that won't mar your work. It's convenient to have two pairs for opening and closing jump rings.

b. Round-nose pliers

Tapered, conical jaws for making loops.

c. Flush cutters

Used for cutting wires and chains. A good pair will leave as little bevel in your cut as possible.

d. Ring mandrel

Used to measure ring size.

e. Measuring tape

Used to measure wire lengths.

f. Bail making pliers

Pliers with cylindrical tips. Mainly used for flat wires in this book, but in general, they can be used for shaping any wire.

g. Nylon jaw pliers

The flat jaws of these pliers are coated, allowing them to straighten wire without leaving marks.

You may also need a coiling tool or a crochet hook depending on your project.

Basic Techniques

Before you get started with the projects in this book, there are a few jewelry making basics you'll want to master first.

USING FLUSH CUTTERS

The jaw blades on flush cutters have a flat side and a convex side. Always cut your wire with the flat side against the wire that you'll be using. That way, any discernible bevel will be left on the spool and not on your work.

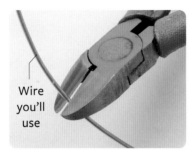
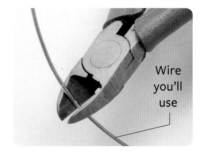

OPENING AND CLOSING JUMP RINGS

You'll need two pairs of chain-nose pliers for this technique. This method can also be used to open and close other round components.

1. With the jump ring facing you, use two pairs of chain-nose pliers to grasp the jump ring on each side of the opening.

2. Push away with one hand and pull toward you with the other hand. Never pull the sides apart, as this will cause the jump ring to become misshapen and you won't be able to make it round again.

3. Close it in the same fashion.

TECHNIQUE 1

Head Pins

TOOLS

✦ Chain-nose pliers
✦ Round-nose pliers
✦ Flush cutters

Head pins are pieces of wire used to hang beads. You can purchase pre-made head pins, but they are actually quite simple to make yourself.

INSTRUCTIONS

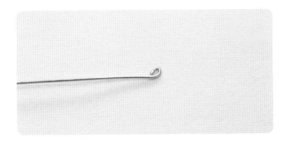

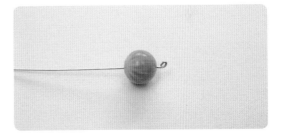

1. Cut a 1½–3 in (4–7.5 cm) piece of wire, depending on the size of your bead. Make a tiny hairpin bend at the tip of the wire and squeeze it closed with chain-nose pliers.

2. String the bead onto the wire.

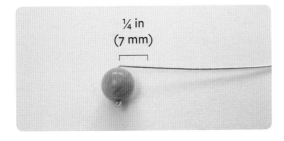

¼ in
(7 mm)

3. Bend the wire to 90 degrees. Cut the excess wire, leaving about ¼ in (7 mm).

4. Grasp the tip of the wire with round-nose pliers.

5. Make a simple loop as you turn the round-nose pliers.

6. Finished head pin charm/dangle.

TECHNIQUE TIPS

- Head pins are used to dangle beads. One end works as a stopper and the other end works as a jump ring.
- You can open and close the simple loop in the same manner as you would a round jump ring (see page 32).
- Recommended gauge: 22 ga or 24 ga.
- Choose a wire gauge as thick as your bead holes can accommodate, since thicker wire is stronger. If 22 ga or 24 ga wire will not pass through your beads, use the wire wrapped loop technique shown on page 37 instead.
- Make the loops in opposite directions on the two ends of the head pin. This configuration makes the head pin stronger.

TECHNIQUE 2

Eye Pins

TOOLS

✦ Chain-nose pliers
✦ Round-nose pliers
✦ Flush cutters

Eye pins are pieces of wire featuring simple loops, which can be used to connect beads and chains.

INSTRUCTIONS

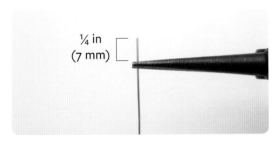

1. Cut a piece of wire the length of your bead plus 1¼ in (3 cm) more. Use chain-nose pliers to bend the wire to 90 degrees about ¼ in (7 mm) from one end.

2. Use round-nose pliers to bend this back into a simple loop.

3. String the bead onto the wire. Bend the remaining wire to 90 degrees.

4. Finish with another simple loop using round-nose pliers.

5. Open and close the loops on the eye pin the same way you do a head pin or jump ring (see page 32). This photo shows two eye pins that have been connected.

TECHNIQUE TIPS

- Since eye pins have simple loops on both sides, you can use them to connect chains or to connect multiple eye pins together.

- Recommended gauge: 22 ga or 24 ga.

- Choose a wire gauge as thick as your bead holes can accommodate, since thicker wire is stronger. If 22 ga or 24 ga wire will not pass through your beads, use the wire wrapped loop technique shown on page 37 instead.

- Make the simple loops in opposite directions on the two ends of the eye pin. This configuration makes the eye pin stronger.

- If you're connecting several eye pin links into a chain, you can attach each new link as you go, attaching the new loop to the previous link in the chain before closing the loop.

TECHNIQUE 3

Wire Wrapped Loops

TOOLS

✦ Chain-nose pliers
✦ Round-nose pliers
✦ Flush cutters

Wire wrapped loops are stronger than simple loops because you wrap the neck to keep them closed.

WIRE WRAPPED LOOPS

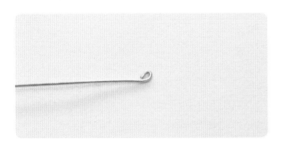

1. Cut a 1½–3 in (4–7.5 cm) piece of wire, depending on the size of your bead. Make a tiny hairpin bend at the tip of the wire and squeeze it closed with chain-nose pliers.

2. String the bead onto the wire.

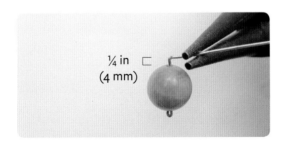

¼ in
(4 mm)

3. Bend the wire to 90 degrees about ¼ in (4 mm) from the bead hole.

4. Begin a loop above the bead.

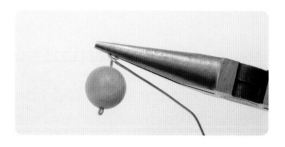

5. Finish the loop by bringing the wire fully around the jaw of the round-nose pliers.

6. Grasp the loop securely with chain-nose pliers.

7. Using your fingers or another pair of chain-nose pliers, grasp the wire and wrap it snugly around the neck twice.

8. Trim the extra wire using flush cutters and pinch the end against the neck with chain-nose pliers.

WIRE WRAPPED LINK

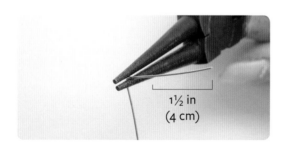

1. Working from the spool, make a 90 degree bend 1½ in (4 cm) from the end.

2. Begin a loop with round-nose pliers.

3. Complete the loop, bringing the wire around the jaw of the round-nose pliers.

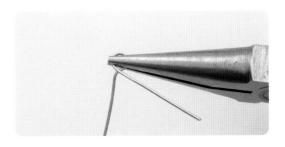

4. Grasp the loop securely with chain-nose pliers.

5. Using your fingers or another pair of chain-nose pliers, grasp the wire and wrap it snugly around the neck twice.

6. Trim the extra wire using flush cutters and pinch the end against the neck with chain-nose pliers.

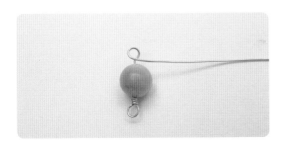

7. Cut the wire from the spool, leaving yourself 1½–3 in (4–7.5 cm), depending on the size of your bead. String the bead onto the wire and make a second loop following steps 3–5 of the Wire Wrapped Loop instructions on pages 37–38.

8. Important: When connecting wire wrapped links, always connect the link you're finishing to the previous link before wrapping the neck.

9. Use chain-nose pliers to grasp the loop, then wrap the wire around the neck twice.

10. Trim the extra wire using flush cutters and pinch the end against the neck with chain-nose pliers.

WIRE WRAPPED LOOP USING BRIOLETTE BEADS

1. Working from the spool, create a wire wrapped loop following steps 1–5 of Wire Wrapped Link instructions on pages 38–39.

2. Trim the extra wire and pinch the end against the neck using chain-nose pliers. Bend at a 45 degree angle.

3. Cut the wire from the spool, leaving yourself about 1 in (2.5 cm). String the briolette onto the wire.

4. Position the bead with the point right under the loop.

5. Bend the wire up on the other side of the bead.

6. Wrap the wire around the neck, starting at the bottom and working up toward the first wraps. Trim the wire when it meets the previous wraps and pinch the end against the neck using chain-nose pliers.

TECHNIQUE TIPS

- Recommended gauge: 24 ga, 26 ga, or 28 ga.
- If you're using jump rings with wire wrapped loops, try to use jump rings that are the same size as the wrapped loops, for consistency.

TECHNIQUE 4
Wire Letters

Create the alphabet with wire! Practice on thin wire and then advance to a thicker gauge.

INSTRUCTIONS

Use round-nose pliers to form the wire into shape, following the lines of the template. Make sure to close the loops and tuck cut ends in on the back.

TECHNIQUE TIPS

- Recommended gauge: 18 ga or 20 ga.
- It's best to work with heavier gauge wire for strength.
- Use chain-nose pliers to connect letters to chains.

TECHNIQUE 5

Lashing

TOOLS

◆ Chain-nose pliers
◆ Round-nose pliers
◆ Flush cutters
◆ Mandrel

Wrap thin wire around a base of thicker wire to cover it with beads.

INSTRUCTIONS

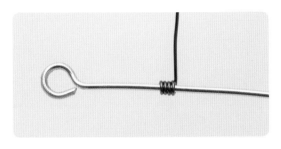

1. Wrap the 28 ga wire tightly around the base wire four times. Pinch the end snugly using chain-nose pliers.

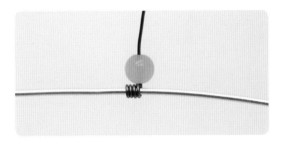

2. String a bead onto the 28 ga wire.

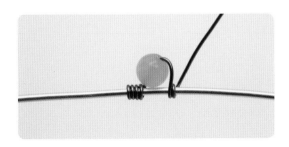

3. Wrap the 28 ga wire around the base wire twice, right next to the bead.

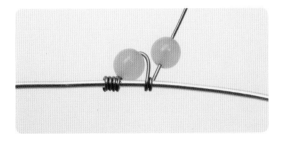

4. String another bead onto the 28 ga wire.

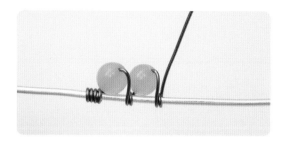

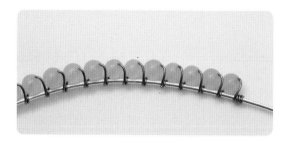

5. Wrap the 28 ga wire around the base wire twice, right next to the bead.

6. Repeat the process until you cover the desired length of the base wire. Wrap the end of the 28 ga wire around the base wire four times, then trim and pinch the end snugly using chain-nose pliers.

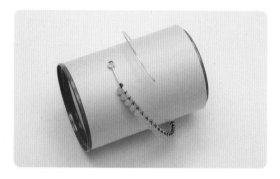

7. Use a mandrel or a can to form the design into shape.

TECHNIQUE TIPS

- Recommended gauge: 18 ga or 20 ga for the base wire and 28 ga for the wrapping wire.
- You can shape the base wire after adding the beads for simple shapes, such as circles for the bangles and earrings on page 75. But make sure to shape the base wire before adding the beads for more complex shapes, such as the heart earrings on page 77.

TECHNIQUE 6

Coiling

TOOLS

✦ Flush cutters
✦ Coiling tool

Use tightly wound coils to embellish plain wire.

INSTRUCTIONS

1. Wrap the end of the wire around the coiling tool a couple of times.

2. Hold the coiling tool and the wire together with your non-dominant hand.

3. Holding the wire against the tool mandrel, turn the handle with your dominant hand, coiling the wire around the mandrel.

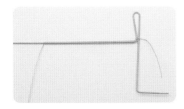

4. Keep coiling until you reach the desired length.

5. Cut the wire from the tool and remove the coil from the mandrel.

TECHNIQUE TIPS

- Recommended gauge: 26 ga, 28 ga, or 30 ga.
- You can cut the coils into smaller sections to decorate headpins.
- A coiling tool with a 1 mm mandrel is used in this book. You can find coiling tools with other diameter mandrels if you wish to change the coil size.

TECHNIQUE 7
Crochet

TOOLS

✦ Crochet hook (select your crochet hook based on your desired loop size)
✦ Flush cutters

So far, we've relied on pliers to form wire into shape. Now let's learn how to create elegant designs using fine wire and a crochet hook.

INSTRUCTIONS

Note: Thicker wire is used in the photos below to help illustrate the technique. Use 28 ga wire for best results.

1. Hold the wire in your non-dominant hand.

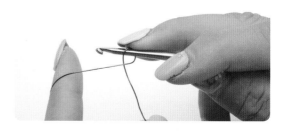

2. Wrap the end of the wire around the index finger, then hold it with the middle finger and thumb.

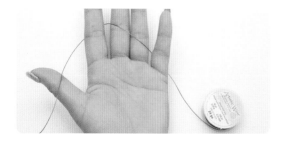

3. Wrap the wire loosely around the hook as indicated by the arrow.

4. This creates your first loop.

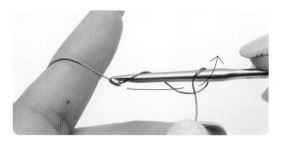

5. Hook the wire on the tip of the crochet hook and pull it back through the loop.

6. This creates a second loop.

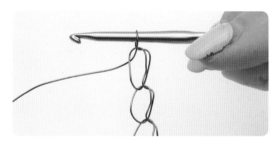

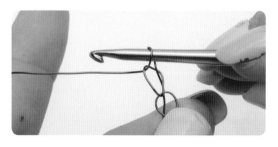

7. Continue pulling the wire through the previous loop.

8. Completed view of step 7. A chain of loops is beginning to form.

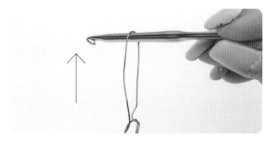

9. Follow this process to make as many loops as necessary.

10. Cut the wire and pull the end through the last loop to end the chain.

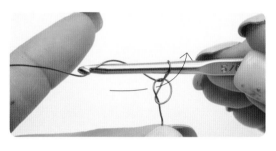

11. Completed view.

Project Instructions

Beaded Charm Bracelets A & D

Shown on page 6

TECHNIQUE

Head Pins

TOOLS

✦ Chain-nose pliers
✦ Round-nose pliers
✦ Flush cutters

FINISHED SIZE

6¼ in (16 cm)

MATERIALS

FOR A (SHOWN OPPOSITE)

✦ 19¾ in (50 cm) of 22 ga tarnish resistant silver craft wire
✦ Five 6 mm yellow chalcedony beads
✦ Three 4 mm purple chalcedony beads
✦ Five 4 mm gold metal stardust beads
✦ 12½ in (32 cm) long silver chain
✦ 6¼ in (16 cm) long gold chain
✦ Nine 3.5 mm round silver jump rings (24 ga)
✦ One silver toggle clasp

FOR D (SHOWN ON PAGE 6)

✦ 19¾ in (50 cm) of 22 ga tarnish resistant brass craft wire
✦ Five 6 mm orange chalcedony beads
✦ Three 4 mm green chalcedony beads
✦ Five 4 mm silver metal stardust beads
✦ 12½ in (32 cm) long gold chain
✦ 6¼ in (16 cm) long silver chain
✦ Nine 3.5 mm round gold jump rings (24 ga)
✦ One gold toggle clasp

INSTRUCTIONS

1. Use flush cutters to cut three 6¼ in (16 cm) long pieces of chain (you'll have two pieces of the main color and one piece of the accent color).

2. Make 13 stone and metal bead dangles on head pins, as shown on page 33.

3. Connect three dangles to the center of one of the main color chains using a jump ring.

4. Use jump rings to connect the remaining dangles to the chain every 10 links. Refer to the photo below for layout.

5. Join the three chains together at each end using two jump rings per end. Before closing the jump rings, attach the toggle ring to one end and the toggle bar to the other end.

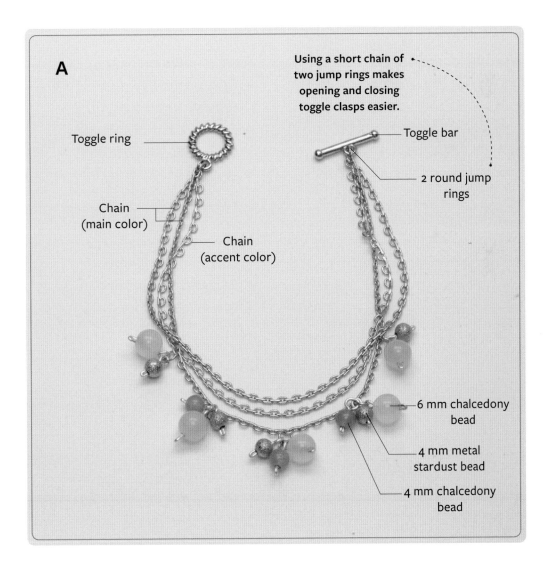

A

Toggle ring

Using a short chain of two jump rings makes opening and closing toggle clasps easier.

Toggle bar

2 round jump rings

Chain (main color)

Chain (accent color)

6 mm chalcedony bead

4 mm metal stardust bead

4 mm chalcedony bead

Beaded Charm Bracelets B & C

Shown on page 6

TECHNIQUE

Head Pins

TOOLS

+ Chain-nose pliers
+ Round-nose pliers
+ Flush cutters

FINISHED SIZE

6¼ in (16 cm)

MATERIALS

FOR B (SHOWN OPPOSITE)

+ 59 in (150 cm) of 24 ga tarnish resistant silver craft wire
+ Ten 2.5–3 mm champagne gold freshwater potato pearls
+ 19 2 mm white button-cut glass beads
+ 6¼ in (16 cm) long silver chain
+ 14 2.3 mm round silver jump rings (24 ga)
+ One silver spring ring clasp
+ One silver extender chain

FOR C (SHOWN ON PAGE 6)

+ 59 in (150 cm) of 24 ga tarnish resistant brass craft wire
+ Ten 2.5–3 mm champagne gold freshwater potato pearls
+ 19 2 mm blue/brown button-cut glass beads
+ 6¼ in (16 cm) long gold chain
+ 14 2.3 mm round gold jump rings (24 ga)
+ One gold spring ring clasp
+ One gold extender chain

1. Cut the chain to size using flush cutters.

2. Make 29 freshwater pearl and glass bead dangles on head pins, as shown on page 33.

3. Using a jump ring for each set, attach sets of two beads or pearls to the chain about every seven links. Refer to the photo below for layout.

4. Attach the spring ring clasp to one end of the chain with a round jump ring.

5. Attach the extender chain to the other end of the chain with a round jump ring.

6. Attach the remaining five dangles to the end of the extender chain.

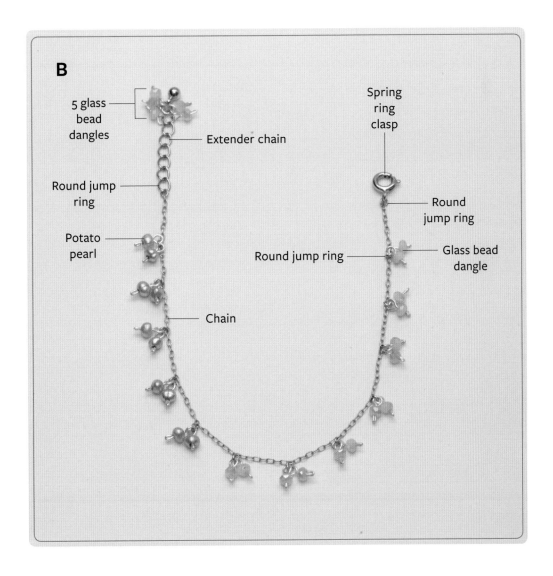

B

5 glass bead dangles

Spring ring clasp

Extender chain

Round jump ring

Round jump ring

Potato pearl

Round jump ring

Glass bead dangle

Chain

Coin Pearl Bracelet

Shown on page 8

TECHNIQUE

Eye Pins

TOOLS

+ Chain-nose pliers
+ Round-nose pliers
+ Flush cutters

FINISHED SIZE

6¾ in (17 cm)

MATERIALS

FOR A (SHOWN OPPOSITE)

+ 15¾ in (40 cm) of 22 ga tarnish resistant silver craft wire
+ Nine 12 mm platinum Swarovski Crystal coin pearls
+ Four 5 mm round silver jump rings (21 ga)
+ One silver toggle clasp

FOR B (SHOWN ON PAGE 8)

+ 15¾ in (40 cm) of 22 ga tarnish resistant brass craft wire
+ Nine 12 mm white Swarovski Crystal coin pearls
+ Four 5 mm round gold jump rings (21 ga)
+ One gold toggle clasp

INSTRUCTIONS

1. Fasten nine pearls with eye pins, as shown on page 35.

2. Connect the nine eye pins.

3. Use a round jump ring to connect one side to the toggle ring.

4. Use the remaining three round jump rings to connect the other side to the toggle bar.

A

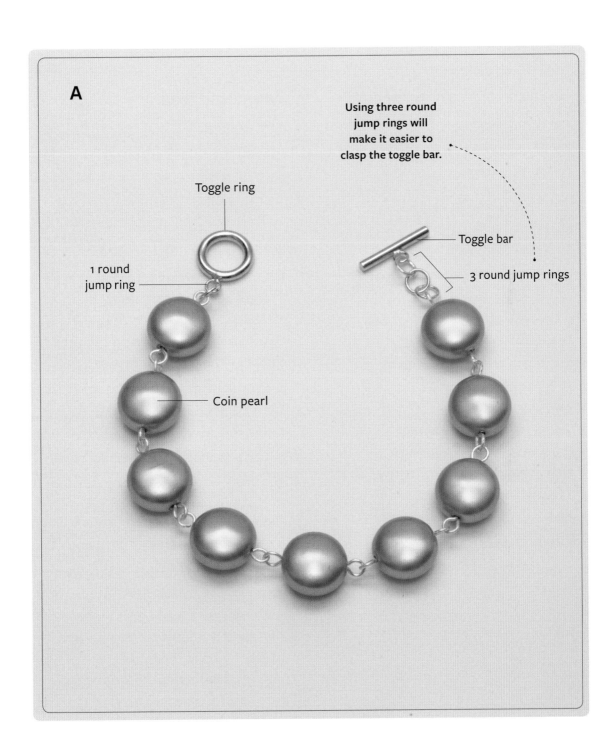

Using three round jump rings will make it easier to clasp the toggle bar.

Toggle ring

Toggle bar

1 round jump ring

3 round jump rings

Coin pearl

Faceted Rondelle Bracelet

Shown on page 9

TECHNIQUE

Eye Pins

TOOLS

+ Chain-nose pliers
+ Round-nose pliers
+ Flush cutters

FINISHED SIZE

6¼ in (16 cm)

MATERIALS

+ 2 in (5 cm) of 22 ga tarnish resistant brass craft wire
+ 2 in (5 cm) of 26 ga tarnish resistant brass craft wire
+ Six 10 mm brown faceted glass rondelle beads
+ Two clear seed beads
+ Two 4 mm gold daisy spacer beads
+ 4¾ in (12 cm) long gold chain
+ Two 5 mm round silver jump rings (21 ga)
+ One gold spring ring clasp
+ One gold extender chain

INSTRUCTIONS

1. String two rondelles, a daisy spacer, a rondelle, a daisy spacer, and then two more rondelles onto the 22 ga craft wire. Make a simple loop on each end to complete the eye pin (see page 35).

2. Cut the chain in half using the flush cutters and attach one piece to each end of the eye pin.

3. Use a round jump ring to connect one side to the clasp.

4. Use a round jump ring to connect the other side to the extender chain.

5. Make a charm for the end of the extender chain by making a simple loop at one end of a 26 ga wire (see page 36), then stringing a seed bead, a rondelle, then another seed bead. Make a wire wrapped loop at the other end (see page 37), connecting the loop to the extender chain before you finish wrapping.

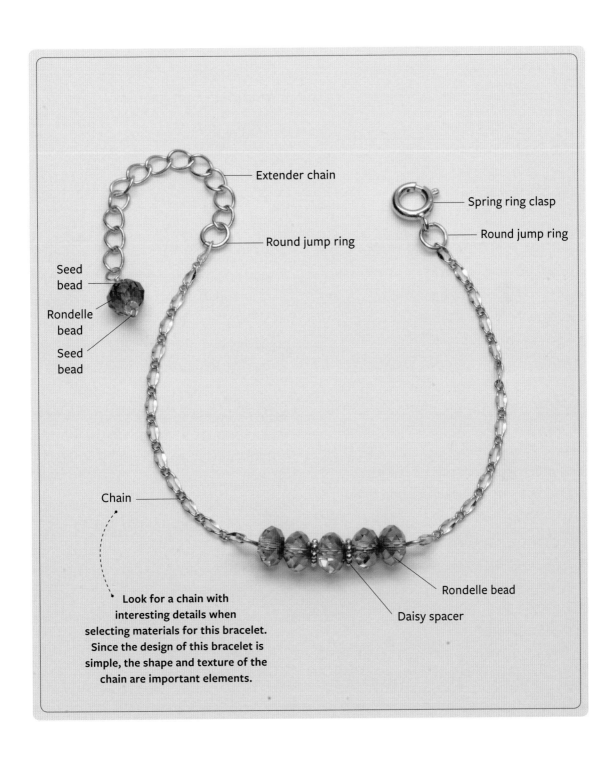

Extender chain

Round jump ring

Spring ring clasp

Round jump ring

Seed
bead

Rondelle
bead

Seed
bead

Chain

**Look for a chain with
interesting details when
selecting materials for this bracelet.
Since the design of this bracelet is
simple, the shape and texture of the
chain are important elements.**

Rondelle bead

Daisy spacer

Pearl Dangle Earrings

Shown on page 10

TECHNIQUE

Wire Wrapped Loops

TOOLS

+ Chain-nose pliers
+ Round-nose pliers
+ Flush cutters

FINISHED SIZE

1¼ in (3 cm)

MATERIALS

FOR A (SHOWN OPPOSITE)

+ 19¾ in (50 cm) of 24 ga tarnish resistant silver craft wire
+ 4 in (10 cm) of 28 ga tarnish resistant silver craft wire
+ Two 7 × 5 mm chrysoprase briolette beads
+ 14 3.5 × 4 mm white freshwater potato pearls
+ One set of 20 mm silver ear wires
+ Four 2.3 mm round silver jump rings (24 ga)

FOR B (SHOWN ON PAGE 10)

+ 19¾ in (50 cm) of 24 ga tarnish resistant brass craft wire
+ 4 in (10 cm) of 28 ga tarnish resistant brass craft wire
+ Two 7 × 5 mm rose quartz briolette beads
+ 14 3.5 × 4 mm white freshwater potato pearls
+ One set of 20 mm gold ear wires
+ Four 2.3 mm round gold jump rings (24 ga)

INSTRUCTIONS

1. Make 14 freshwater pearl dangles with wire wrapped loops using the 24 ga wire, as shown on page 37.

2. String two pearl dangles onto a round jump ring. Repeat for the remaining three jump rings.

3. Make two briolette dangles with wire wrapped loops using the 28 ga wire, as shown on page 40.

4. String all the components onto the ear wire in the order shown in Figure 1 on page 57. Repeat for the second earring.

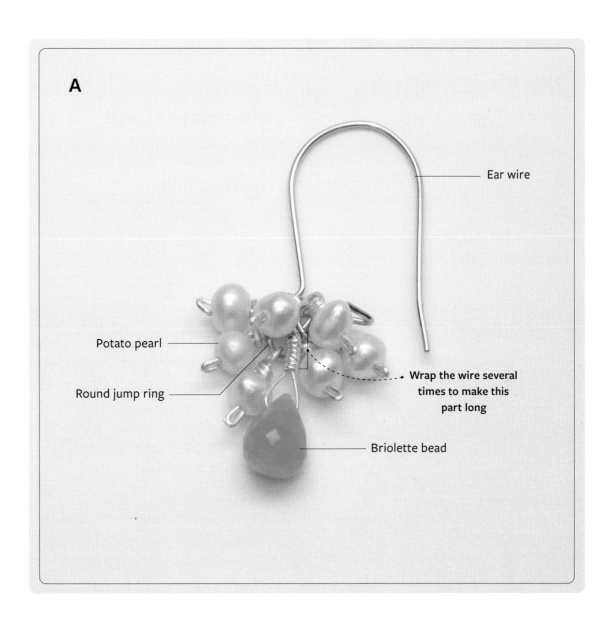

A

Ear wire

Potato pearl

Round jump ring

Wrap the wire several times to make this part long

Briolette bead

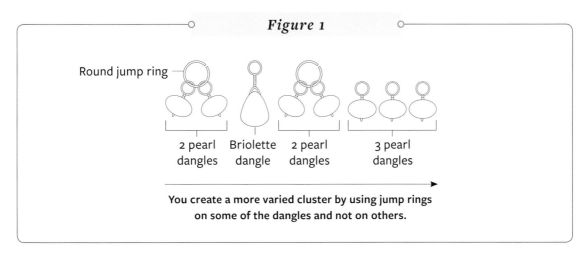

Figure 1

Round jump ring

2 pearl dangles

Briolette dangle

2 pearl dangles

3 pearl dangles

You create a more varied cluster by using jump rings on some of the dangles and not on others.

Milk Glass Necklace

Shown on page 11

TECHNIQUE

Wire Wrapped Loops

TOOLS

✦ Chain-nose pliers
✦ Round-nose pliers
✦ Flush cutters

FINISHED SIZE

15¾ in (40 cm)

MATERIALS

FOR A (SHOWN OPPOSITE)

✦ 2⅜ in (6 cm) of 26 ga tarnish resistant silver craft wire
✦ One 20 × 8 mm pink Czech glass bead
✦ 15 in (30 cm) long silver chain
✦ One silver spring ring clasp
✦ One silver extender chain
✦ Four 2.3 mm round silver jump rings (24 ga)

FOR B (SHOWN ON PAGE 11)

✦ 2⅜ in (6 cm) of 26 ga tarnish resistant brass craft wire
✦ One 20 × 8 mm white Czech glass bead
✦ 15 in (30 cm) long gold chain
✦ One gold spring ring clasp
✦ One gold extender chain
✦ Four 2.3 mm round gold jump rings (24 ga)

INSTRUCTIONS

1. Make a wire wrapped link using the Czech glass bead, and connect each end to a round jump ring. Be sure to not finish wrapping the loops until you've connected the loop to the jump ring, as shown on pages 38–40.

2. Cut the chain into two 7½ in (19 cm) lengths using the flush cutters.

3. Connect each piece of chain to one of the round jump rings from step 1.

4. Using a round jump ring on each end, attach the spring ring to one side of the chain, and the extender chain to the other side.

A

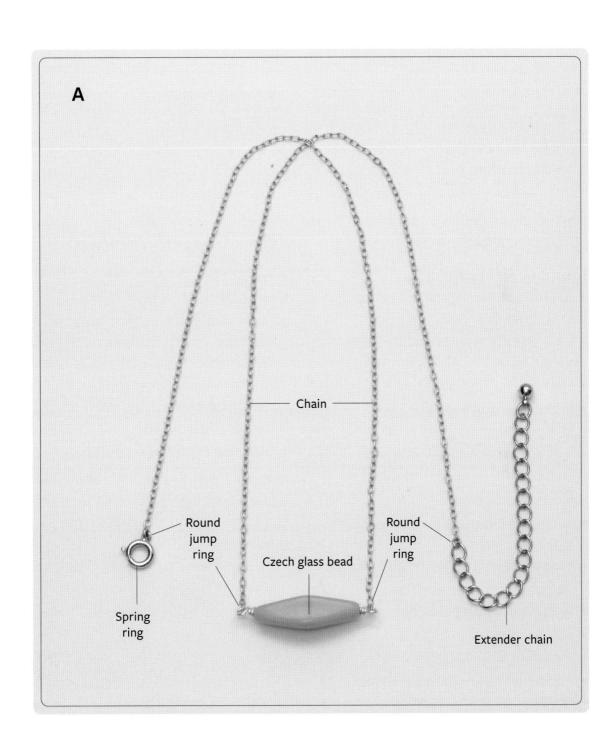

Chain

Round jump ring

Czech glass bead

Round jump ring

Spring ring

Extender chain

Stacked Shell Necklace

Shown on page 11

TECHNIQUE

Wire Wrapped Loops

TOOLS

✦ Chain-nose pliers
✦ Round-nose pliers
✦ Flush cutters

FINISHED SIZE

15¾ in (40 cm)

MATERIALS

FOR C (SHOWN OPPOSITE)

✦ 4 in (10 cm) of 26 ga tarnish resistant brass craft wire
✦ 2 in (5 cm) of 3 mm brown shell heishe beads
✦ 15 in (34 cm) long gold chain
✦ One gold spring ring clasp
✦ One gold extender chain
✦ Two 2.3 mm round gold jump rings (24 ga)

FOR D (SHOWN ON PAGE 11)

✦ 4 in (10 cm) of 26 ga tarnish resistant silver craft wire
✦ 2 in (5 cm) of 3 mm gray shell heishe beads
✦ 15 in (34 cm) long silver chain
✦ One silver spring ring clasp
✦ One silver extender chain
✦ Two 2.3 mm round silver jump rings (24 ga)

INSTRUCTIONS

1. Cut the chain into two 6¾ in (17 cm) lengths using the flush cutters.

2. Make a wire wrapped link using the shell heishe beads, and connect the ends to both pieces of chain. Be sure to not finish wrapping the loops until you've connected the loop to the chain, as shown on pages 38–40.

3. Bend the link into a slight curve.

4. Using a round jump ring on each end, attach the spring ring to one side of the chain, and the extender chain to the other side.

C

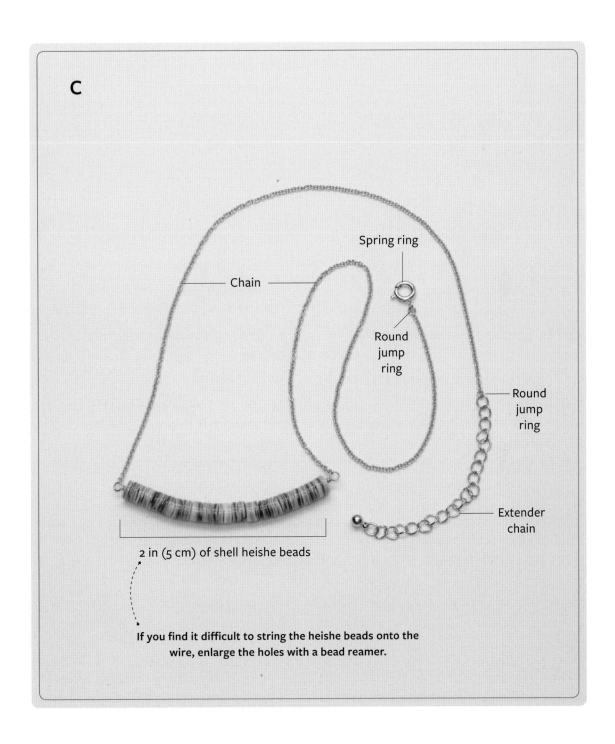

Spring ring

Chain

Round jump ring

Round jump ring

Extender chain

2 in (5 cm) of shell heishe beads

If you find it difficult to string the heishe beads onto the wire, enlarge the holes with a bead reamer.

Gemstone Kaleidoscope Necklace

Shown on page 12

TECHNIQUE

Wire Wrapped Loops

TOOLS

✦ Chain-nose pliers
✦ Round-nose pliers
✦ Flush cutters

FINISHED SIZE

33½ in (85 cm)

MATERIALS

FOR A (SHOWN ON PAGE 12)

✦ 43¼ in (110 cm) of 24 ga tarnish resistant silver craft wire
✦ 13 12 mm blue agate faceted round beads
✦ 14 6 mm pink coral round beads
✦ 16 8 mm white coral round beads
✦ Two 40 × 16 mm silver metal links
✦ One silver toggle clasp
✦ Five 5 mm round silver jump rings (20 ga)

FOR B (SHOWN OPPOSITE)

✦ 43¼ in (110 cm) of 24 ga tarnish resistant brass craft wire
✦ 13 12 × 10 mm turquoise flat round beads
✦ 14 15 × 12 mm yellow jade teardrop beads
✦ 16 8 mm white coral round beads
✦ Two 40 × 16 mm gold metal links
✦ One gold toggle clasp
✦ Five 5 mm round gold jump rings (20 ga)

INSTRUCTIONS

1. Connect all the beads with wire wrapped links, as shown on page 38. Refer to the photo at right for layout.

2. Connect the metal links where shown, using jump rings on the ends without holes.

3. Use two round jump rings to connect the toggle bar to one side of the necklace, then use the remaining round jump ring to connect the toggle ring to the other side.

B

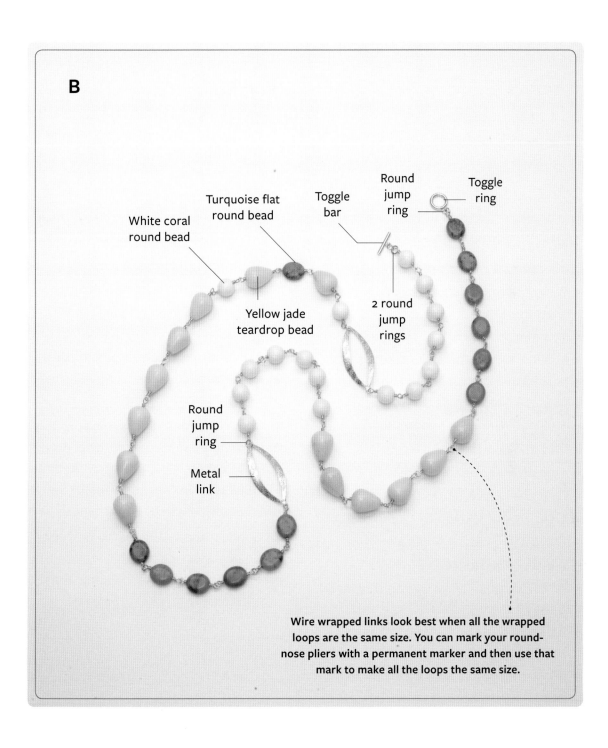

White coral round bead

Turquoise flat round bead

Toggle bar

Round jump ring

Toggle ring

Yellow jade teardrop bead

2 round jump rings

Round jump ring

Metal link

Wire wrapped links look best when all the wrapped loops are the same size. You can mark your round-nose pliers with a permanent marker and then use that mark to make all the loops the same size.

Double Strand Necklace

Shown on page 13

Shown on page 13

TECHNIQUE

Wire Wrapped Loops

TOOLS

✦ Chain-nose pliers
✦ Round-nose pliers
✦ Flush cutters

FINISHED SIZE

40½ in (103 cm)

MATERIALS

FOR A (SHOWN OPPOSITE)

✦ 8 yds (7.4 m) of 26 ga tarnish resistant silver craft wire
✦ 13 4 mm pyrite white round beads
✦ 15 2 mm pyrite white round beads
✦ 25 4 mm white coral round beads
✦ 35 2 mm white coral round beads
✦ 28 4 mm peridot round beads
✦ 28 2 mm peridot round beads
✦ One silver spring ring clasp
✦ One silver chain tab
✦ Eight 2.3 mm round silver jump rings (24 ga)

FOR B (SHOWN ON PAGE 13)

✦ 8 yds (7.4 m) of 26 ga tarnish resistant brass craft wire
✦ 66 4 mm champagne gold freshwater pearls
✦ 78 2 mm champagne gold freshwater pearls
✦ One gold spring ring clasp
✦ One gold chain tab
✦ Eight 2.3 mm round gold jump rings (24 ga)

INSTRUCTIONS

1. Randomly connect the 4 mm beads with wire wrapped links, as shown on page 38, until you have a 15 in (38 cm) length and an 11 in (28 cm) length.

2. Randomly connect the 2 mm beads with wire wrapped links, until you have two 13½ in (34 cm) lengths.

3. Connect both strands from step 2 with two jump rings on each end. Attach one side to the 15 in (38 cm) length of 4 mm beads and the other side to the 11 in (28 cm) length of 4 mm beads.

4. Connect the spring ring to one end of the necklace and the chain tab to the other end using two round jump rings on each end.

A

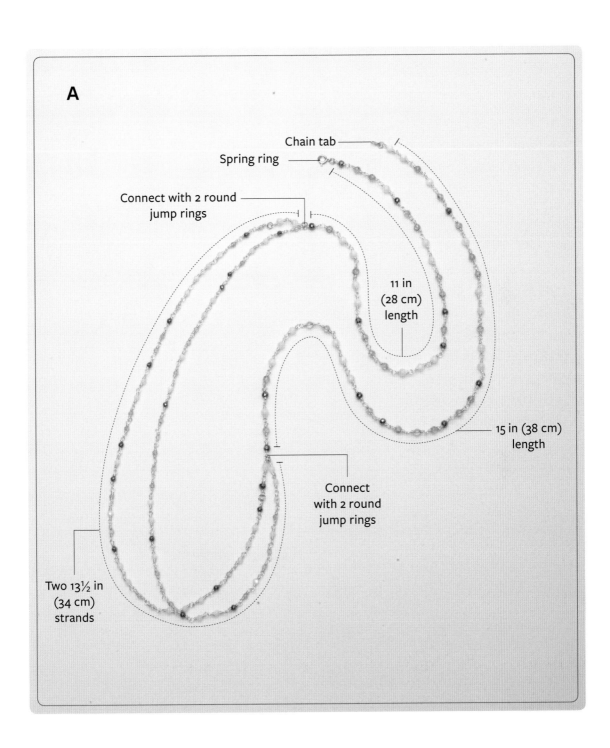

Chain tab

Spring ring

Connect with 2 round jump rings

11 in (28 cm) length

15 in (38 cm) length

Connect with 2 round jump rings

Two 13½ in (34 cm) strands

Pearl Choker

Shown on page 14

TOOLS

✦ Chain-nose pliers
✦ Round-nose pliers
✦ Flush cutters

TECHNIQUE

Thick Wire

FINISHED SIZE

12¾ in (32 cm)

MATERIALS

✦ 13¾ in (35 cm) of 18 ga tarnish resistant brass craft wire
✦ 2 in (5 cm) of 20 ga tarnish resistant brass craft wire
✦ One 12 mm white pearl (a cotton pearl was used in the sample on page 14)

Pearl ——

INSTRUCTIONS

1. String the pearl onto the 20 ga wire and form it into a head pin (see page 33).

2. Bend one end of the 18 ga wire into a simple loop, just as when making an eye pin (see page 35).

3. String the pearl head pin from step 1 onto the 18 ga wire.

4. On the other end of the 18 ga wire, begin to make a simple loop, but do not close it completely. This becomes the hook. Refer to the step-by-step photos of this process pictured below.

5. Shape the wire into a choker.

6. Close the choker with the hook and simple loop.

How to Make Hooks

1. Use round-nose pliers to bend the wire to 90 degrees about ¾ in (2 cm) from the end.

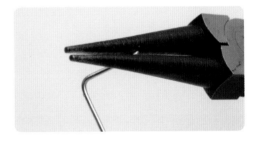

2. Bend the wire back to begin a simple loop.

3. Do not close the loop completely. Use a metal file to smooth the end of the hook if necessary.

Metal Bangle

Shown on page 15

TECHNIQUE

Thick Wire

TOOLS

- ✦ Chain-nose pliers
- ✦ Round-nose pliers
- ✦ Flush cutters

FINISHED SIZE

7 in (18 cm)

MATERIALS

FOR A (SHOWN BELOW)

- ✦ 15¾ in (40 cm) of 20 ga tarnish resistant brass craft wire
- ✦ 4 in (10 cm) of 28 ga tarnish resistant silver craft wire
- ✦ One 10 mm gold metal bead
- ✦ Two 10 mm silver metal beads
- ✦ Six 6 mm gold metal rondelle beads
- ✦ Four 4 mm silver metal rondelle beads

FOR B (SHOWN ON PAGE 15)

- ✦ 15¾ in (40 cm) of 20 ga tarnish resistant silver craft wire
- ✦ 4 in (10 cm) of 28 ga tarnish resistant silver craft wire
- ✦ One 10 mm gold metal bead
- ✦ Two 6 mm silver metal rondelle beads
- ✦ Two 4 mm gold metal rondelle beads

INSTRUCTIONS

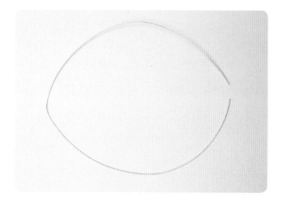

1. Match up the ends of the 20 ga wire.

2. Bring the sides of the wire together, leaving an open loop at the fold.

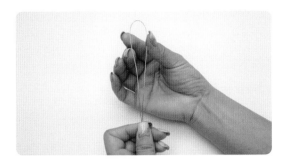

3. Bend the wire into a bangle.

4. String the beads onto both wires in the order shown. Refer to the photo on page 15 for B. Make sure to string the beads onto the wire first as you cannot put them on after making the hook.

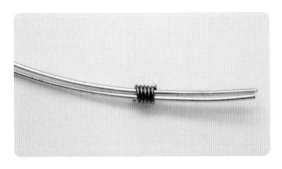

5. Tightly wrap the 28 ga wire around both wires five times about ¾ in (2 cm) from the end. Trim the wire and pinch snugly with chain-nose pliers. Note: A different color is used for the 28 ga wire for illustration purposes.

6. Use chain-nose pliers to make a bend just after the wraps from step 5. Repeat step 5 about ¼ in (5 mm) from the end.

7. Bend the last ¼ in (5 mm) of the 20 ga wire over on itself using chain-nose pliers.

8. Use round-nose pliers to curve the wires into a hook shape between the wraps.

Charming Wrap Bracelets

Shown on page 17

TECHNIQUE

Wire Letters

TOOLS

+ Chain-nose pliers
+ Round-nose pliers
+ Flush cutters
+ Beading needle

FINISHED SIZE

31½ in (80 cm) total

MATERIALS

FOR A (SHOWN OPPOSITE)

+ 6 in (15 cm) of 20 ga tarnish resistant brass craft wire
+ 220 11/0 brown seed beads
+ 90 11/0 tan seed beads
+ 100 11/0 white seed beads
+ 80 11/0 light blue seed beads
+ 45 11/0 pink seed beads
+ One gold spring ring clasp
+ One gold extender chain
+ Two gold crimp beads
+ Four 4 mm round gold jump rings (20 ga)
+ 39½ in (100 cm) of white beading wire

FOR B (SHOWN ON PAGE 17)

+ 6 in (15 cm) of 20 ga tarnish resistant silver craft wire
+ 500 11/0 dark gray seed beads
+ 35 11/0 silver seed beads
+ One silver spring ring clasp
+ One silver extender chain
+ Two silver crimp beads
+ Four 4 mm round silver jump rings (20 ga)
+ 39½ in (100 cm) of white beading wire

INSTRUCTIONS

1. Use round-nose pliers to make four letters, following the templates on page 71.

2. Use a beading needle to string all the seed beads onto the beading wire. Refer to the layout on page 71 for A and the photo on page 17 for B. The strung beads should measure 31½ in (80 cm).

3. String on a crimp bead and the spring ring, then thread the end of the beading wire back through the crimp bead.

4. Crush the crimp bead using chain-nose pliers, thread the tail through several beads, then trim the excess.

5. Follow the same process to install a crimp bead and extender chain on the other end of the bracelet.

6. Make a seed bead dangle with a wire wrapped link, as shown on pages 38–40. Don't finish wrapping the loops until you've connected the loop to the extender chain.

7. Use round jump rings to connect the letters to the center of the bracelet/ necklace at ⅜ in (1 cm) intervals.

A

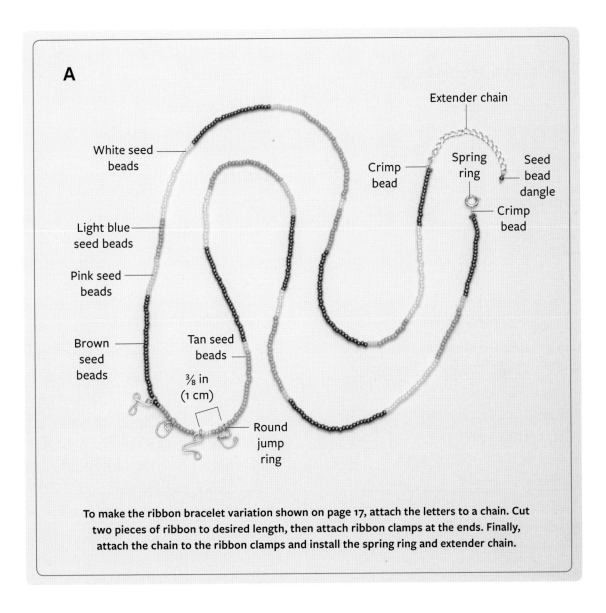

White seed beads

Light blue seed beads

Pink seed beads

Brown seed beads

Tan seed beads

⅜ in (1 cm)

Round jump ring

Extender chain

Crimp bead

Spring ring

Seed bead dangle

Crimp bead

To make the ribbon bracelet variation shown on page 17, attach the letters to a chain. Cut two pieces of ribbon to desired length, then attach ribbon clamps at the ends. Finally, attach the chain to the ribbon clamps and install the spring ring and extender chain.

Templates

These templates are designed for 20 ga wire, which is used for the projects in this section. If using 18 ga wire, you'll need to enlarge the templates slightly.

Mantra Necklaces

Shown on page 18

TECHNIQUE

Wire Letters

TOOLS

✦ Chain-nose pliers
✦ Round-nose pliers
✦ Flush cutters

FINISHED SIZE

2½ in (6.5 cm) for the wire letters

MATERIALS

FOR A (SHOWN OPPOSITE)

✦ 8 in (20 cm) of 20 ga tarnish resistant brass craft wire
✦ 2 in (5 cm) of 24 ga tarnish resistant brass craft wire
✦ Two 3.5 × 4 mm white freshwater potato pearls
✦ One 10 mm gold metal heart charm
✦ 12¾ in (32 cm) gold chain
✦ One gold spring ring clasp
✦ One gold extender chain
✦ Four 4 mm round gold jump rings (20 ga)

FOR B (SHOWN OPPOSITE)

✦ 8 in (20 cm) of 20 ga tarnish resistant silver craft wire
✦ 2 in (5 cm) of 24 ga tarnish resistant silver craft wire
✦ Two small navy glass beads
✦ One 10 mm gold metal star charm
✦ 12¾ in (32 cm) silver chain
✦ One silver spring ring clasp
✦ One silver extender chain
✦ Four 4 mm round silver jump rings (20 ga)

INSTRUCTIONS

1. Use round-nose pliers and the 20 ga wire to make the word, following the templates on page 73.

2. Make a freshwater pearl or navy glass bead dangle with 24 ga wire, using a wire wrapped loop as shown on page 37.

3. Use flush cutters to cut two 6¼ in (16 cm) long pieces of chain.

4. Connect one chain to the loop at the beginning of the word with a round jump ring. Connect the spring ring to the end of that chain with another round jump ring.

5. Connect the other chain to the loop at the end of the word with a round jump ring. Before closing the jump ring, string on the metal charm and the dangle from step 2.

6. At the other end of that chain, connect the extender chain using a round jump ring. Make and attach another dangle to the extender chain before you finish wrapping the loops.

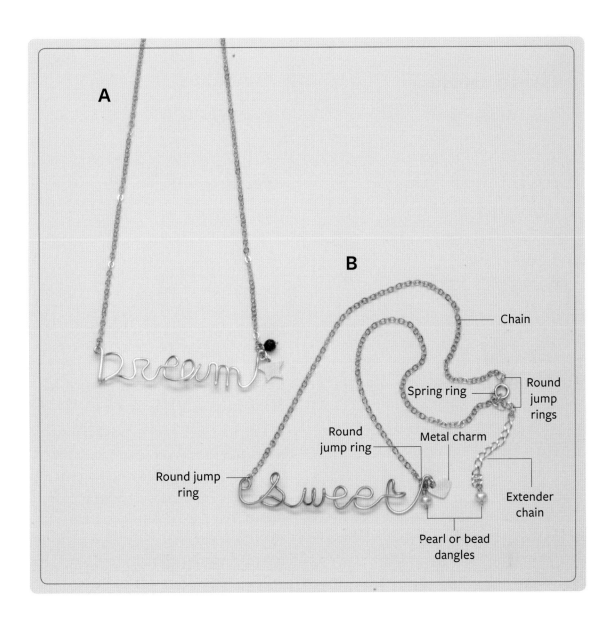

A

B

Chain

Spring ring

Round jump rings

Round jump ring

Metal charm

Round jump ring

Extender chain

Pearl or bead dangles

Templates

These templates are designed for 20 ga wire, which is used for the projects in this section. If using 18 ga wire, you'll need to enlarge the templates slightly.

Lashed Bangles

Shown on page 19

Shown on page 19

TECHNIQUE

Lashing

TOOLS

- Chain-nose pliers
- Round-nose pliers
- Flush cutters
- Mandrel (or a can)

FINISHED SIZE

7 in (18 cm)

MATERIALS

- 8 in (20 cm) of 20 ga tarnish resistant silver craft wire
- 27½ in (70 cm) of 28 ga tarnish resistant silver craft wire
- 24 11/0 blue seed beads
- 24 11/0 yellow seed beads

INSTRUCTIONS

1. Make a hook and a loop on each end of the 20 ga wire (see page 67).

2. Use the 28 ga wire to begin lashing the seed beads 1½ in (4 cm) from the loop (see page 43). Refer to the photo on page 19 for bead layout. Stop 1½ in (4 cm) from the hook on the other end of the bracelet.

3. Shape the bangle using a can for a mandrel.

To make the circular lashed earrings shown below, use round-nose pliers to make a loop on one end and a gentle hook on the other end of each piece of 20 ga wire. File the end of the hook to make it smooth. Use the lashing technique on page 43 to add the beads to each earring.

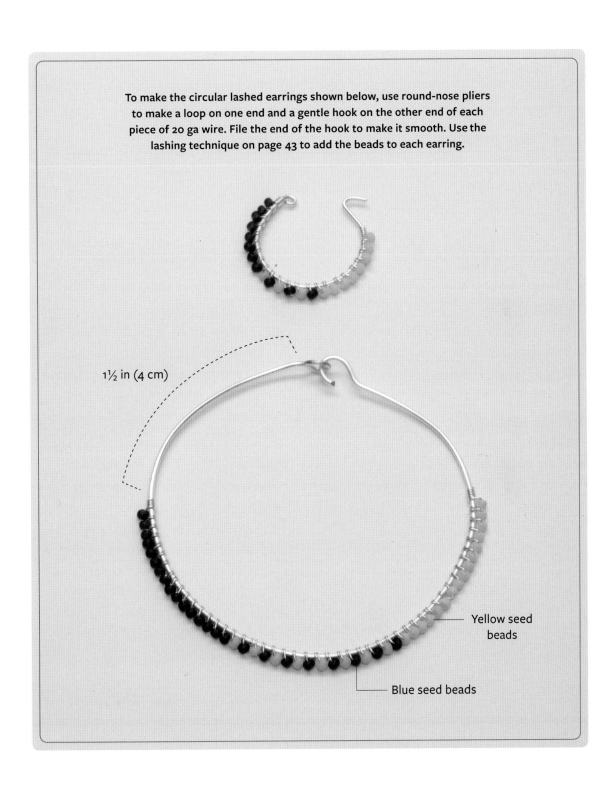

1½ in (4 cm)

Yellow seed beads

Blue seed beads

Lashed Earrings

Shown on page 19

TECHNIQUE

Lashing

TOOLS

✦ Chain-nose pliers
✦ Round-nose pliers
✦ Flush cutters

FINISHED SIZE

1½ in (4 cm)

MATERIALS

✦ 16 in (40 cm) of 20 ga tarnish resistant silver craft wire
✦ 31½ in (80 cm) of 28 ga tarnish resistant silver craft wire
✦ 100 2 mm white freshwater potato pearls
✦ Two 5 mm round silver jump rings (24 ga)
✦ Silver ear wires

INSTRUCTIONS

1. Cut two 8 in (20 cm) pieces of 20 ga wire and bend each one into a heart shape. Make small loops at the ends using round-nose pliers and fasten them together. A marker makes a good mandrel for bending the wire into the heart shape.

2. Use the 28 ga wire to begin lashing the pearls at the point marked by the arrow in the photo on page 77 (see page 43 for lashing instructions). You'll be working around the heart in a clockwise direction. Wrap the 28 ga wire around the base wire three times for each pearl, except for the beginning, end, and areas next to the V-shape at the top of the heart. Wrap the 28 ga wire around the base wire five times for those pearls.

3. Attach the ear wires with round jump rings.

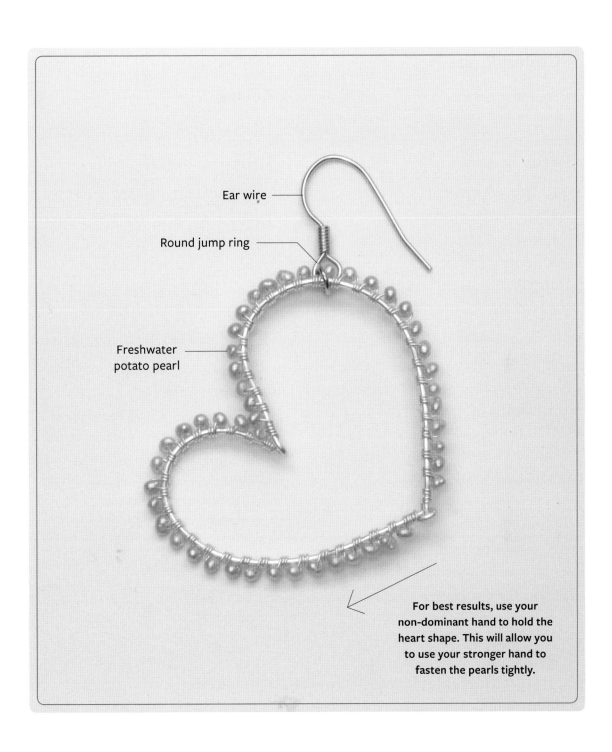

Ear wire

Round jump ring

Freshwater
potato pearl

For best results, use your
non-dominant hand to hold the
heart shape. This will allow you
to use your stronger hand to
fasten the pearls tightly.

Coiled Rings

Shown on page 21

TECHNIQUE

Coiling

TOOLS

✦ Chain-nose pliers
✦ Round-nose pliers
✦ Flush cutters
✦ Coiling tool

FINISHED SIZE

Size 6 (Adjust the lengths of coil and wire to suit desired ring size)

MATERIALS

FOR ALL

✦ 4 in (10 cm) of 24 ga tarnish resistant silver craft wire
✦ 39½ in (100 cm) of 28 ga tarnish resistant silver craft wire

FOR A (SHOWN OPPOSITE)

✦ 12 3 mm powder almond Swarovski Crystal pearls (#5810)

FOR B (SHOWN ON PAGE 21)

✦ 12 3 mm white Swarovski Crystal pearls (#5810)

FOR C (SHOWN OPPOSITE)

✦ 5 4 mm black diamond Swarovski Crystal faceted round beads (#5000)

FOR D (SHOWN ON PAGE 21)

✦ 5 4 mm crystal Swarovski Crystal faceted round beads (#5000)

INSTRUCTIONS

1. Make a 1¼ in (3 cm) long coil using 28 ga wire (see page 45).

2. Thread the 24 ga wire through the coil twice for A and B, stringing on the pearls as shown in Figure 1 on page 79. For C and D, you'll only need to thread the 24 ga wire through the coil once when stringing on the beads.

3. Trim the leftover wire after wrapping it twice in between the coil and the pearls. Pinch the ends snugly with chain-nose pliers.

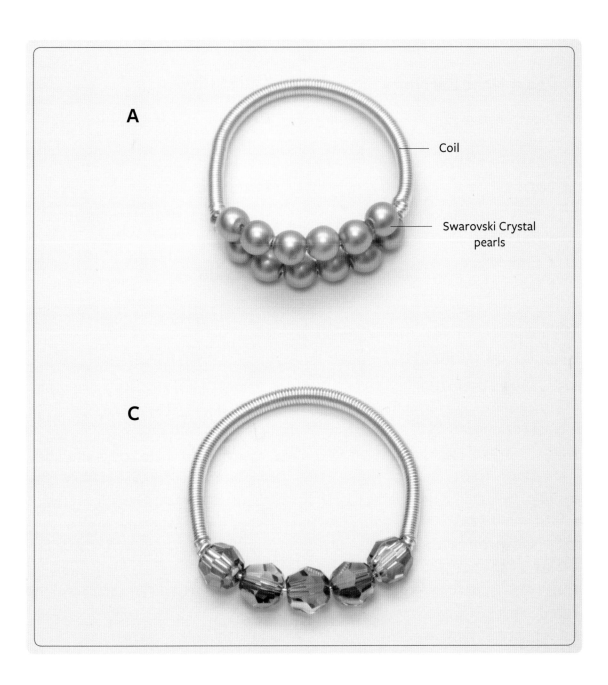

A

Coil

Swarovski Crystal
pearls

C

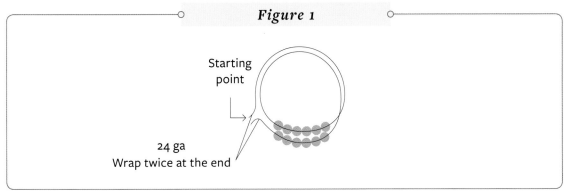

Figure 1

Starting
point

24 ga
Wrap twice at the end

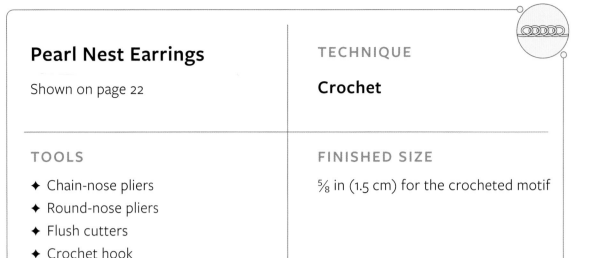

Pearl Nest Earrings

Shown on page 22

TOOLS

+ Chain-nose pliers
+ Round-nose pliers
+ Flush cutters
+ Crochet hook

TECHNIQUE

Crochet

FINISHED SIZE

⅝ in (1.5 cm) for the crocheted motif

MATERIALS

FOR A (SHOWN OPPOSITE)

+ 4 in (10 cm) of 22 ga tarnish resistant brass craft wire
+ 4½ yds (4 m) of 28 ga tarnish resistant brass craft wire
+ Two 10 mm white cotton pearls
+ Gold ball post ear wires

FOR B (SHOWN ON PAGE 22)

+ 4 in (10 cm) of 22 ga rose gold craft wire
+ 4½ yds (4 m) of 28 ga rose gold craft wire
+ Two 10 mm white cotton pearls
+ Gold ball post ear wires

FOR C (SHOWN ON PAGE 22)

+ 4 in (10 cm) of 22 ga tarnish resistant silver craft wire
+ 4½ yds (4 m) of 28 ga tarnish resistant silver craft wire
+ Two 10 mm white cotton pearls
+ Silver screw back non-pierced earring findings
+ 2 in (5 cm) long silver chain
+ Two 4 mm round silver jump rings (24 ga)

INSTRUCTIONS

1. Crochet a 15¾ in (40 cm) long chain with 28 ga wire (see page 46). Leave a short tail on both ends.

2. Spiral the crocheted chain into a nest shape and fasten the tail ends together (refer to Figure 1 on page 81).

3. Place the pearl into the nest.

4. Make a small hook on the end of a 2½ in (6.5 cm) long piece of 22 ga wire. Push the other end through the bottom of the nest, then through the pearl and out the top side of the nest.

5. Close the hook around the crocheted wire on the bottom of the nest.

6. Use the top of the 22 ga wire to make a wrapped loop and connect it to the ear wire.

A

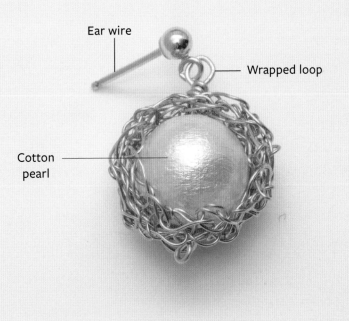

Ear wire

Wrapped loop

Cotton pearl

For variation C, cut the chain into two 1 in (2.5 cm) long pieces.
For each earring, attach one end of the chain to the wrapped loop from step 6, and
then use a jump ring to attach the other end of the chain to the earring finding.

Figure 1

Spiral a crocheted
chain into a nest,
leaving wire tails on
both ends.

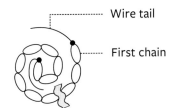

Wire tail

First chain

Flat Wire Rings

Shown on page 23

TECHNIQUE

Flat Wire

TOOLS

- Chain-nose pliers
- Round-nose pliers
- Flush cutters
- Marker
- Ring mandrel

FINISHED SIZE

Sample shown is size 5½
(see step 5 on page 83 for details
about adjusting ring size)

MATERIALS

- 2¾ in (7 cm) of 21 ga gold flat wire
- 11¾ in (30 cm) of 28 ga gold craft wire
- One 10 mm round white freshwater pearl

INSTRUCTIONS

Note: A different color of 28 ga wire is used in the photos to help illustrate the technique.

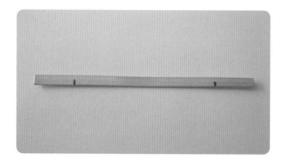

1. Make a mark ½ in (12 mm) from each end on the flat wire.

2. Using round-nose pliers, make a simple loop that ends at the mark you made in step 1.

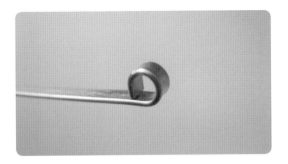

3. Completed loop.

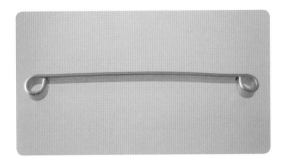

4. Repeat on the other end, making sure both loops are on the same side of the flat wire.

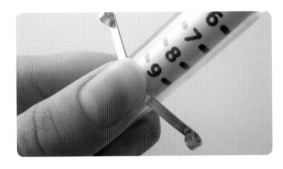

5. Use a ring mandrel to shape the wire into a ring shank: Wrap it around a size that is two sizes smaller than the desired finished size. This makes the shank fully round. Next, slide it down the mandrel to the desired finished size.

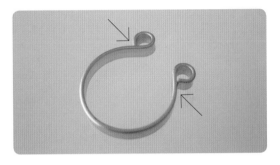

6. Open both loops slightly using chain-nose pliers. This will allow you to wrap the 28 ga wire around the shank.

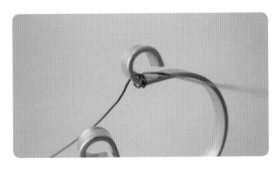

7. Wrap the middle of an 8 in (20 cm) piece of 28 ga wire around one shank loop four times.

8. Bring both ends of the wire together.

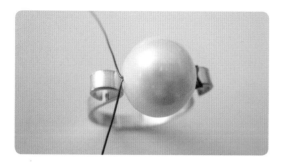

9. String the pearl onto both wires, centering the pearl between the loops of the shank. On the other side, separate the wires on each side of the shank loop.

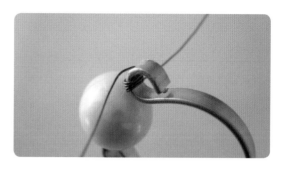

10. Wrap both 28 ga wires around the loop twice.

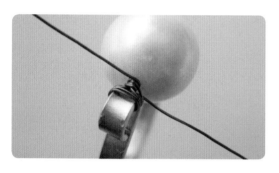

11. Trim the wires and pinch them snugly against the wraps with chain-nose pliers.

12. Use chain-nose pliers to close the loops on the shank.

13. The ring is complete.

TIPS

- When working with flat wire, using nylon-jaw pliers will help eliminate marks made by regular pliers. Also, you may find it easier to use bail making pliers rather than small round-nose pliers, as flat wire is tougher to bend.

- When cutting flat wire, make one forceful cut, rather than slowly squeezing the flush cutters.

Twisted Bangles

Shown on page 23

TECHNIQUE

Flat Wire

TOOLS

+ Flat-nose pliers (2 pairs)
+ Round-nose pliers
+ Flush cutters
+ Nylon-jaw pliers
+ Bail making pliers

FINISHED SIZE

6¾ in (17 cm)

MATERIALS

+ 16¼ in (41.2 cm) of 21 ga gold flat wire

INSTRUCTIONS

1. Use a marker to measure and mark the flat wire at the intervals shown. Be sure to mark both ends, extending out from the center of the wire.

Center

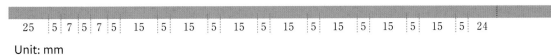

| 25 | 5 | 7 | 5 | 7 | 5 | 15 | 5 | 15 | 5 | 15 | 5 | 15 | 5 | 15 | 5 | 15 | 5 | 15 | 5 | 24 |

Unit: mm

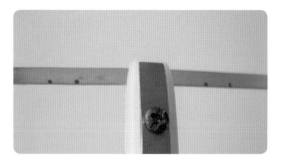

2. Grasp the center of the wire with nylon-jaw flat pliers and bend it into a U-shape.

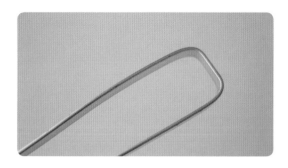

3. U-shaped bend.

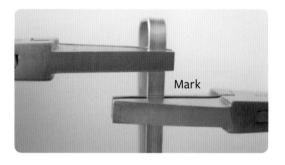

Mark

4. Grasp the first two marks with flat-nose pliers.

5. Twist the wire by holding the top pliers in place and turning the bottom pliers.

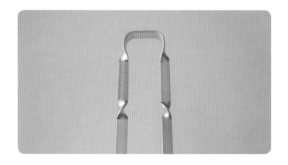

6. Twist the wire just 90 degrees at the marks closest to the center. Twist the wire 180 degrees at the subsequent marks. Make sure both sides are symmetrical.

7. The side with marks will be the front.

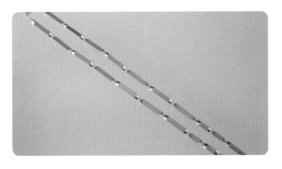

8. Follow the same process to twist the wire at the rest of the marks.

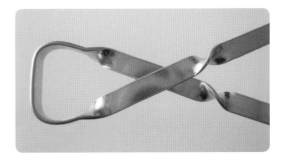

9. Cross the wires between the first and second twists.

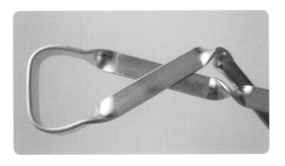

10. Bend the top wire at the twist to cross under the bottom wire.

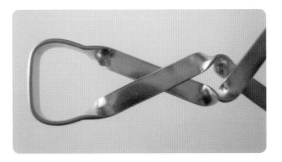

11. Next, bend the bottom wire at the twist to cross over the other wire.

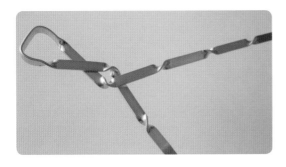

12. Crossed wires.

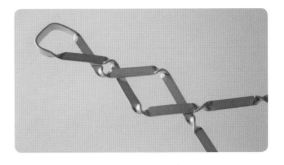

13. Continue bending the wires at the twists and crossing them over each other.

14. Diamond shapes will form from crossing the wires.

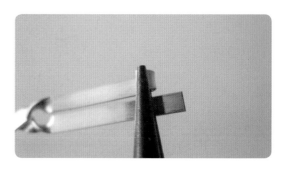

15. Using round-nose pliers, make very small loops on both ends.

16. Completed view of the loops.

17. Pinch the loops closed using nylon-jaw pliers.

18. Completed view of the closed loops.

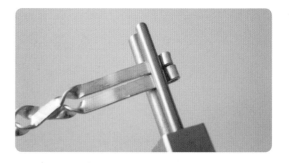

19. Make a hook using bail making pliers.

20. Use bail making pliers to grasp the two wires at the base of the loops. Turn the pliers to the right, with the loops on the outside, to form a hook.

21. Completed view of the hook.

22. Use nylon-jaw pliers to shape the wire into a bangle.

TIP

Flat-nose pliers have square flat jaws. It's easier to use flat-nose pliers on flat wire as they have a larger grasping area than chain-nose pliers.

Wrapped Pendant A

Shown on page 24

Classic Wire Wrap

TOOLS

+ Chain-nose pliers
+ Round-nose pliers
+ Flush cutters
+ Bail making pliers
+ Masking tape

FINISHED SIZE

1¼ in (3 cm)

MATERIALS

+ 11¾ in (30 cm) of 20 ga tarnish resistant brass square wire
+ 4¾ in (12 cm) of 20 ga tarnish resistant silver fancy square wire
+ 19¾ in (50 cm) of 22 gauge tarnish resistant brass half round wire
+ One 18 × 13 mm quartz cabochon

INSTRUCTIONS

1. Cut the tarnish resistant brass square wire into one 6 in (15 cm) long piece (A) and one 4¾ in (12 cm) long piece (C). Arrange A–C as shown below (B is the tarnish resistant silver fancy square wire). Mark the center point on all three wires. Then mark 1¼ in (33 mm) from the ends on both sides of B and mark 1⅜ in (35 mm) from the ends on both sides of C.

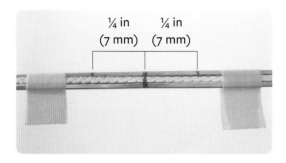

2. Align the center marks and tape the wires together as shown. Mark ¼ in (7 mm) from the center on both sides of the bundle.

3. Cut an 8 in (20 cm) long piece of half round wire and wrap to the ¼ in (7 mm) mark on each side (½ in [14 mm] total). Pinch each wrap snugly against the bundle of wire with chain-nose pliers.

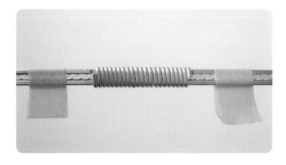

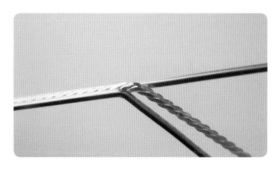

4. Trim any excess on the side with the marks and press in the ends.

5. Bend B and C outward at the marks made in step 1. They should bend toward the side without the marks.

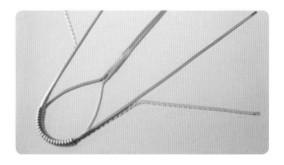

6. Curve the wrapped section around the bottom curve of the cabochon, aligning the centers.

7. Next, curve C around the cabochon, bringing the bends together behind the stone. Tape the wires together above the bend to create a back support for the stone.

8. Shape B around the outside of the cabochon.

9. Tape B and C together temporarily with masking tape. Cut a 6 in (15 cm) long piece of half round wire and wrap B and C four times at the top of the pendant.

10. Remove all masking tape. Bend both sides of C out at about a 30 degree angle. Bend both sides of A up at a 90 degree angle at the end of the wrapped wire section.

11. Bend both sides of A 90 degrees again to form a small step.

12. Place the cabochon into the pendant. Curve both sides of A around the top of the stone. Make marks where the wires come together.

13. Cut a 6 in (15 cm) long piece of half round wire and wrap the two sides of A four times at the mark. Trim the ends and press them snugly against the wires.

14. Bend both sides of A out to the sides and bring B and C together.

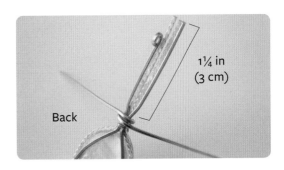

15. Trim B and C to 1¼ in (3 cm) from the neck and curl all of them to the back, making a small loop. Wrap each end of A around the neck once.

16. Completed view of the small loop made with B and C.

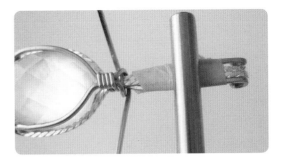

17. Wrap the bundle of wire with masking tape to protect it. Using bail making pliers, bend the bundle of wires to the front creating a bail.

18. Completed bail.

19. Cut one side of A to 1 in (2.5 cm) and the other side to ¾ in (2 cm).

20. Create a spiral on each wire using round-nose pliers.

21. Bend each one toward the front of the bail.

22. Completed pendant.

TIP

The classic wire wrap technique provides a way to capture stones without holes, such as cabochons. You can surround them with wires as shown here, or fasten them with prongs as shown on pages 95–99.

Wrapped Pendant B

Shown on page 24

TOOLS

+ Chain-nose pliers
+ Wide flat-nose pliers
+ Round-nose pliers
+ Flush cutters
+ Masking tape

FINISHED SIZE

1¼ in (3 cm)

MATERIALS

+ 11¾ in (30 cm) of 20 ga tarnish resistant brass square wire
+ 4¾ in (12 cm) of 20 ga tarnish resistant brass fancy square wire
+ 23¾ in (60 cm) of 22 gauge tarnish resistant brass half round wire
+ One 18 × 13 mm quartz cabochon

INSTRUCTIONS

1. Cut the tarnish resistant brass square wire into one 6¾ in (17 cm) long piece (A) and one 4¾ in (12 cm) long piece (C). You'll also need a 4¾ in (12 cm) long piece of tarnish resistant brass fancy square wire (B).

A: 6¾ in (17 cm)

B: 4¾ in (12 cm)

C: 4¾ in (12 cm)

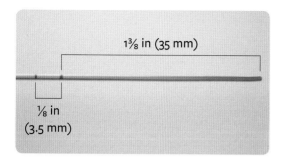

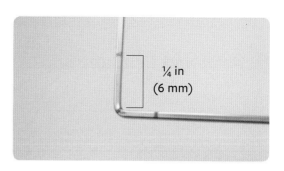

2. Mark A 1⅜ in (35 mm) from one end. Make a second mark ⅛ in (3.5 mm) away.

3. Bend the wire at a 90 degree angle. Place your cabochon next to the wire to determine its height and make a mark slightly above the top of the stone (¼ in [6 mm] in this example). This will be the length of your prongs.

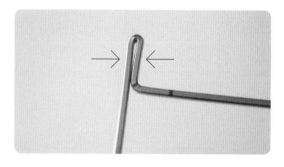

4. Bend the wire at a 90 degree angle at the mark made in step 3.

5. Continue to bend the wire into a complete hairpin bend and pinch it snugly together to form the first prong.

6. Repeat to make a second prong ½ in (13.5 mm) from the first one. Then repeat to make two more prongs following the measurements noted at right.

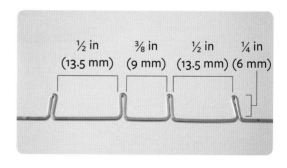

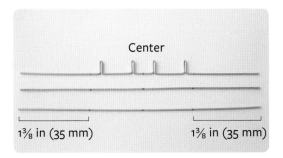

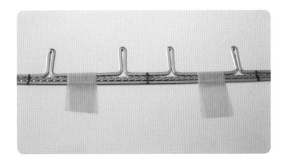

7. On all three wires, mark the center points and 1⅜ in (35 mm) from each end.

8. Arrange A–C as shown above, with the prongs at the top. Tape them together.

9. Hold an 8 in (20 cm) long piece of half round wire at its mid-point and wrap snugly in both directions between the two middle prongs. Cross the wire to the other side of each prong and wrap twice. Trim and pinch the ends against the bundle.

10. Using a 6 in (15 cm) long piece of half round wire, wrap four times from the outside mark next to an outer prong. Cross over the prong and wrap twice. Trim and pinch the ends against the bundle. Repeat on the other outer prong.

11. Bend all the wires at the ends of the wraps, to about 30 degrees.

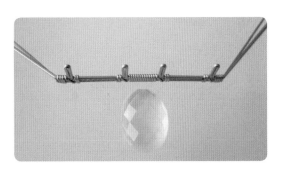

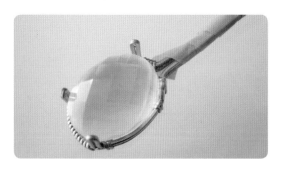

12. Holding the center of the bundle against the bottom of the cabochon, bend all the wires around the stone. Bend the wires up at the top of the stone using chain-nose pliers.

13. Tape all the wires together above the stone. Check to ensure the stone fits.

14. Remove the stone and the masking tape, and using chain-nose and flat-nose pliers, begin bending the prongs over the base.

15. Continue bending the prongs, while testing that the stone fits.

16. With the stone in place, and prongs bent over, tape all six wires together temporarily.

17. Wrap all six wires using a 6 in (15 cm) long piece of half round wire and bend A out to the sides.

18. Bring the other four wires together and trim them evenly.

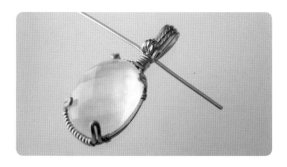

19. Make the bail as shown in steps 15–17 on page 93.

20. Trim each side of A to ¾–1 in (2–2.5 cm), create a spiral using round-nose pliers, and fold them to the front of the bail.

21. Completed pendant.

Ribbon Pendant

Shown on page 25

TECHNIQUE

Classic Wire Wrap

TOOLS

- ✦ Chain-nose pliers
- ✦ Round-nose pliers
- ✦ Flush cutters
- ✦ Bail making pliers
- ✦ Two pins
- ✦ Masking tape

FINISHED SIZE

1¼ in (3 cm)

MATERIALS

- ✦ A: 12 in (30 cm) of 20 ga tarnish resistant silver square wire
- ✦ B: 6 in (15 cm) of 20 ga tarnish resistant silver fancy square wire
- ✦ C: 12 in (30 cm) of 22 gauge tarnish resistant silver half round wire
- ✦ D: 6 in (15 cm) of 22 ga tarnish resistant silver craft wire
- ✦ E: 24 in (60 cm) of 28 ga tarnish resistant silver craft wire
- ✦ F: 12 in (30 cm) of 30 ga tarnish resistant silver craft wire

- ✦ One 12 × 10 mm top-drilled white freshwater pearl
- ✦ One 6 mm round white freshwater pearl
- ✦ Two 5 mm round white freshwater pearls
- ✦ Two 4 mm round white freshwater pearls
- ✦ 12 2.5 mm round freshwater pearls
- ✦ Three 3 mm round silver jump rings (24 ga)
- ✦ Four 4 mm round silver jump rings (24 ga)
- ✦ 18–20 in (45.5–51 cm) long silver chain
- ✦ One silver spring ring clasp
- ✦ One silver extender chain

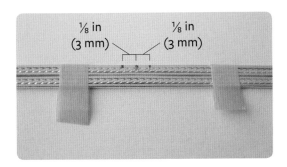

1. Cut four pieces of A, each 2¾ in (7 cm) long. Cut two pieces of B, each 2¾ in (7 cm) long. Tape the six wires together in this order: 1 A, 1 B, 2 A, 1 B, 1 A. Mark the center of the bundle, then mark ⅛ in (3 mm) from the center on each side.

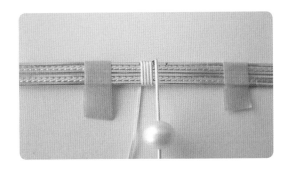

2. Leaving a 3 in (8 cm) tail, wrap C around the bundle from the left mark toward the center mark. String on a 6 mm pearl and continue wrapping to the other mark.

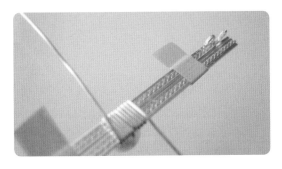

3. Flip the whole bundle and curl in all the ends on both sides using round pliers.

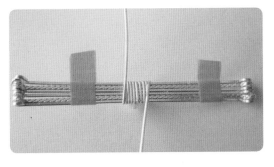

4. Completed view of the curled ends.

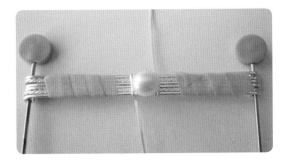

5. Insert a pin through each end to prevent the wires from sliding around, and put masking tape around the bundle to protect the wires from getting scratched.

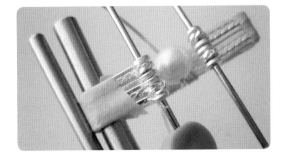

6. Bend each end toward the center on the front side using bail making pliers.

7. Thread the tails of the wrapping wire through the loops on each end.

8. Split each side of the wire bundle to create a bow shape.

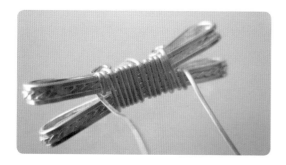

9. Wrap the tail wires around the top and bottom halves of the bow, then trim on the back. Pinch the ends snugly against the bundle.

10. Make a briolette loop with D and the top-drilled pearl (see pages 40–41). String the 2.5 mm pearls onto F as shown in Figure 1 on page 103. Wrap the strung beads around the top of the briolette and anchor them with the wire tails. Trim the tails.

11. Cut E in half. Fold one 12 in (30 cm) long piece in half and hook it around a wire on the back of the bow. String a 4 mm and 5 mm pearl on to both wires. Repeat on the other side with the other 12 in (30 cm) long piece of wire.

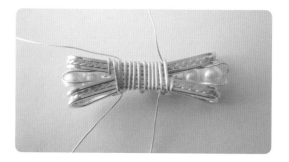

12. Bring the wires to the back of the bow and pull the two wires to opposite sides of the pendant. Do the same on the other side.

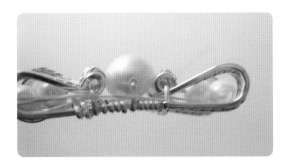

13. Wrap each of the E tails around C twice. Trim and pinch them snugly against the bundles.

4 mm round jump ring

Three 3 mm round jump rings

14. Connect the briolette loop from step 10 to the pendant using three 3 mm round jump rings. Cut the chain in half. Connect each piece of chain to the pendant using 4 mm round jump rings. Connect the clasp and extender chain using 4 mm round jump rings as well.

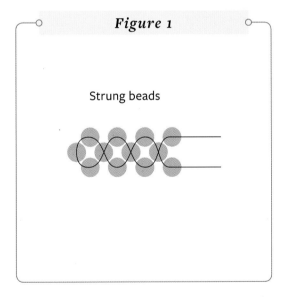

Figure 1

Strung beads

TIP

You can make round jump rings to match your jewelry. Make a coil of matching wire and cut the rings of wire using flush cutters. Make sure that you cut both ends with the flush side of the cutters. That ensures you can close the jump rings snugly.

Resources

ARTISTIC WIRE

www.beadalon.com

FIRE MOUNTAIN GEMS

www.firemountaingems.com

FUSION BEADS

www.fusionbeads.com

HOBBY LOBBY

www.hobbylobby.com

JOANN

www.joann.com

LIMA BEADS

www.limabeads.com

MICHAELS

www.michaels.com

RINGS & THINGS

www.rings-things.com

RIO GRANDE

www.riogrande.com